The Case of the Hidden Masterpiece

Phyllis J. Perry

Illustrations by Ron Lipking

Fort Atkinson, Wisconsin

For Michelle and Matt, who make everything possible.

Published by UpstartBooks
W5527 State Road 106
P.O. Box 800
Fort Atkinson, Wisconsin 53538-0800
1-800-448-4887

Copyright © 2006 by Phyllis J. Perry
Cover and interior illustrations © 2006 by Ron Lipking

The paper used in this publication meets the minimum requirements of American National Standard for Information Science — Permanence of Paper for Printed Library Material. ANSI/NISO Z39.48.

I like mysteries—things that disappear, spooky noises in the night, and unexpected happenings. So when Mom came home from the grocery store and said she'd met our old friend Mrs. Carabell, and that Mrs. Carabell was terribly worried because her cat was missing, I instantly went on alert. A strange disappearance. Aha! If I'd had antennae tucked in among my spiky red hair, they'd have been fully extended and bobbing about.

My two buddies in my fifth grade class at Hennessey Elementary School, Aaron and Mike (who we called Dynamike), would be coming to my house any minute now for a game of Monopoly®. But instead of playing a game, I suddenly had other ideas. I finished helping Mom put the groceries away, popped a piece of gum in my mouth, and then drummed my fingers idly on the kitchen counter.

Aaron and Dynamike arrived on my doorstep and I stepped outside before they even rang the bell. "Hey, want to help me solve a mystery?"

"What's up, Wink?" said Dynamike using my nick-name, which was short for my last name, Winklehockey. He looked eager to hear more. I don't think he had been looking forward any more than I had to a game of Monopoly. It had been Aaron's idea to play of course. Dynamike and I both knew there'd be no contest. Aaron would win. He always won.

Aaron was tall, had blonde hair, was a great student, and was a born entrepreneur. Some day he'd run a big corporation. Maybe Dynamike and I would even work for him. In the meantime, we had a mystery to solve.

"Mrs. Carabell's cat is missing," I explained. "Maybe we can help her find it."

"Now?" Aaron asked. "I thought we were going to play Monopoly."

"Well, we could wait, I guess, but top-notch investigators try to get on a case right away, before the trail goes cold."

"Since when did we become top-notch investigators?" Aaron asked.

"You didn't think we'd be second-rate, did you?" I asked innocently.

"I didn't know we were investigators at all." Aaron was beginning to look kind of exasperated.

"Why not form an agency?" Dynamike piped up. He was the shortest boy in the fifth grade, but what he lacked in size, he made up for in enthusiasm. Right now his eyes were sparkling. Action and adventure appealed to him a lot more than Monopoly. "Wink is always looking for mysteries anyway. Why not solve one?"

"Right," I agreed. "We can bike over to Mrs. Carabell's and find out what happened. And then we can offer to get on the case."

Aaron sighed loudly, but I think he was only pretending to make a sacrifice in giving up his game. I knew he loved puzzles and mysteries, too. "And what's the name of our top-notch agency?" he asked. "Just in case Mrs. Carabell should ask?"

Sometimes Aaron could be a little sarcastic. But knowing that Dynamike was firmly on my side, I plunged ahead.

"We do need a name," I agreed. "Let's look in the phone book and see what some private investigating agencies call themselves."

We tromped into the kitchen where Mom kept a phone book on a shelf beneath the phone. Quickly I turned to the yellow pages.

"What do you suppose you look under?" Dynamike asked.

"Private Investigators, I guess." I opened the book and ran my finger down the pages, "Printers, Printing, Printing Supplies, Process Servers. Hmmm. No Private Investigators."

"Try Investigators," Aaron suggested.

I flipped open the pages again and moved my finger down each listing: Insurance, Interior Decorators, International Trade Consultants, Internet Services, Investigators. "Here it is," I said. "Here's one that specializes in manned, remote, and body-worn video surveillance. They're called Thornton Research. We could be Winklehockey Research Associates, I guess."

"Not exactly a catchy name," Aaron pointed out.

It sounded pretty good to me, but I didn't argue. "Here's Beston & Woods and Burton & Associates," I continued. "This isn't too helpful. Mostly they just use their last names."

"How about Private Eye Spy?" Dynamike suggested.

Aaron groaned. "We can do better than that, I hope."

"Let's see." I started muttering our names aloud while I thought. "Dynamike, Aaron, Wink-DAW, Mike, Aaron, Wink-MAW-Wink, Aaron Mike-WAM-Winklehockey." Then inspiration struck. "How about—the WHAM Agency?"

"WHAM? How'd you come up with that?" Dynamike asked.

"Sounds pretty powerful, huh?" I said. "Packs a punch. The 'WH' is from my name, Winklehockey, the 'A' is for Aaron, and the 'M' is for you, Mike. What do you think?"

"The WHAM Agency," Aaron said it aloud twice. "Not bad."

"Sounds great to me," Dynamike agreed. "So let's go. I'm ready for the WHAM Agency's first case."

I led the way, and my dog, Bugle, followed us as we biked to Mrs. Carabell's house. We left our bikes on the lawn and climbed the steps. I rang the bell and waited.

Mrs. Carabell looked surprised to find the three of us on her front porch.

"Hello, boys," she said, brushing back a wisp of white hair that had slipped down on her forehead. "I haven't seen you around lately. Is there a problem with your tree house?"

More than a year ago, Mrs. Carabell had let us build a platform that we called Raven's Roost in a tree in the vacant lot she owned right next to her house. We used scrap lumber and made a pretty neat perch about fifteen feet off the ground.

"No, ma'am," I answered quickly. "No problem. It's about your missing cat. We thought you might need the services of the WHAM Agency."

"The WHAM Agency?"

"Right," I said. "We're private investigators."

"Oh, of course," Mrs. Carabell answered, looking from one to the other of us. "I should have guessed. Why don't you come in, boys, and we'll talk business."

"Right," I said again, thinking that old Mrs. Carabell was still pretty sharp. When I told Bugle to "stay," he gave a whine of discontent but quickly settled down on his stomach to wait just outside the door.

Mrs. Carabell led the way into her sitting room, which was filled with antique furniture and lacy pillows. Several well-worn books rested on the coffee table. There was a spicy smell in the air and I wondered what it was. Cinnamon cookies? As I looked around at the plush couch and the little white crocheted pieces on the chair backs and arms, I knew it was a room in which no gum had ever been chewed. With a gulp, I swallowed mine.

Mrs. Carabell took off her apron and went to the kitchen. Aaron sank into a soft cushion of the couch, and Mike perched on a spindly-legged chair with a red velvet seat. I noticed that he sat very still with his elbows close to his body as if he was afraid he might break something. I felt the same way. In that room, one good sneeze might cause a million small figurines to topple and splinter on the ground.

"Could I offer you boys some milk and cookies?" Mrs. Carabell called from the kitchen.

I saw the smile that immediately appeared on Dynamike's face. He was small, but he always had a huge appetite.

"No, thank you," I said regretfully, and watched the grin fade from Dynamike's face. It was a real sacrifice, but I decided that accepting cookies wouldn't be very businesslike.

As Mrs. Carabell returned, I used what I hoped was an efficient investigative approach. "We'd like a few facts, ma'am." I pulled from my pocket the stubby pencil and small spiral notebook I always carried. "Now, what's your cat's name and when was the last time that you saw it?"

Mrs. Carabell settled into a rocking chair. "Her name is Fortune. She's a rare shaded-silver Persian; she's all white, but the tip of each hair is silver gray. Her eyes are emerald green, and she's a real beauty."

I scribbled down "white" and "green eyes."

"I know that she came out into the garden with me last Saturday morning after breakfast. I can't say that I actually saw her after that. I got busy with my work, and didn't pay any more attention to her."

I wrote, "Fortune last seen, one week ago, Saturday morning."

"She's expecting kittens about now, which is why I'm so worried. She usually delivers her kittens in a box in my empty garage. They're always so beautiful, it's very easy to find good homes for them." She paused for a moment and I saw her eyes glisten. "You know, I've never kept one for myself. But now I wish I had. I may never see Fortune again."

For a moment, I was afraid that Mrs. Carabell might bawl. But she pulled herself together and continued. "She's been a wonderful companion for five years. And she never misses her supper. Even if she's been outside wandering about, she always appears on the back steps at five o'clock every night." Mrs. Carabell fell quiet.

"But last Saturday was different?" I prodded.

"When I went out back to let her in, she wasn't there. I couldn't believe it. I actually came back inside and phoned Time and Temperature. I thought it was more likely that my clock was wrong than that Fortune would miss supper. But it really was five o'clock, and no cat. I checked for her every half hour, but she never came home."

I scribbled another note.

"Believe me, I spent a sleepless night. I got up twice and went out back to look again by moonlight. I tried to tell myself that she'd be waiting on the doorstep and extra hungry Sunday morning, but when I woke up last Sunday and went outside, Fortune was nowhere to be seen. It's been a week now, and I'm terribly worried. I call the Humane Society every day, but no one has brought her in."

Aaron asked, "Did you notice anyone suspicious hanging around your house last Saturday?"

"Not suspicious, no. While I was out raking leaves in the yard, I saw some teenagers I didn't recognize. Three girls with backpacks. One had that kind of radio you young folks love to carry around. She was playing it awfully loud. That's how I happened to look up and notice them."

"Could you describe the girls?" I asked.

"Yes. There was a pair of twins with long blonde hair. You don't often see twins, so they stood out. I'd recognize them again. The other girl, who carried the radio, had short brown hair, but I'm afraid I didn't get a real good look at her. Does that help?"

"It sure does," Aaron said. I could tell by his voice that he was excited. "I have a sister in middle school," he went on. "She's talked about the Patterson twins. I'll bet that's who you saw. We can look them up in the phone book and see where they live."

"But what have the twins got to do with the cat?" asked Dynamike.

"Maybe nothing, maybe everything," I answered, trying to sound very wise. What was wrong with Dynamike anyway? Spotting twins sounded like a perfectly good clue to me, and I wasn't about to spoil it. "Could we borrow your phone book, Mrs. Carabell?"

"Of course." She hurried to get it, and brought it to us.

"There are too many Pattersons to call them all up," Aaron decided after running his finger down a long list. He closed the book. "I guess we'll have to go home and ask my sister if she knows where the twins live."

We stood up to leave. "We'll report back to you, Mrs. Carabell, as soon as we learn something," I said. "And try not to worry. The WHAM Agency is on the job."

She smiled. "I feel better already."

Bugle greeted us on the front porch with wild tail wagging as if we'd been gone for months instead of minutes. He trotted along beside us as we biked back down the street to Aaron's house.

"Our first case!" I observed proudly.

Luckily Aaron's sister was home and knew that the Patterson twins, Brittany and Beth, lived on Grant Street. We looked up the address, and I wrote it with their phone number in my notebook.

"Now what do we do?" Aaron asked.

"We don't have a lot of time before dinner, but I think we should go over to the Pattersons instead of phoning. It's not far, and it'd be better to do this face-to-face," I said.

"Shouldn't we at least call and tell them we're coming over?" Dynamike asked.

I shook my head. "Better to take them by surprise before they have time to try to cook up a story."

"Cook up what story?" Dynamike looked puzzled. I ignored him.

A minute later, we were speeding off to Grant Street.

When Aaron rang the bell, a blonde girl answered the door. She looked at the three of us and the dog. "Well," she asked, "what are you guys selling?"

Bugle wagged his tail in a friendly way. "Sit," I commanded.

"We're not selling anything," Aaron answered. "Are you Beth or Brittany?"

"Beth," she replied. She looked surprised that he knew her name.

"I'm Aaron Bates. My sister, Meg, gave us your address."

"Oh, sure. You're Meg's little brother." I noticed Aaron cringe when she said that. "She talks about you all the time. What do you want?"

"We're investigating a case," I said, stepping forward. "And we have a couple of questions we'd like to ask you and your sister."

"A case?" Beth said. "Come on in." She looked puzzled but led us into the living room and called upstairs. "Brittany! Come on down."

Brittany came down the stairs. "These guys have some questions to ask us," Beth explained as Brittany sat next to her on the couch.

"Mrs. Carabell's our client," Aaron began. "She's pretty old and lives all alone except for her cat, Fortune, who's lost. Mrs. Carabell reports that last Saturday when the cat disappeared, twins walked by her house. We wondered if you were the twins, and if you know anything about a missing cat."

To my surprise, an identical expression crossed the girls' faces, and they looked at one another. Until this moment, I hadn't really thought there was any connection between the twins and the cat. But now I knew there must be. They looked guilty.

Brittany was the first to speak. "We feel awful about it, but we didn't know what to do. So we didn't do anything."

I pulled out my notebook. "You'd better tell us what happened."

After fidgeting for a moment, Beth finally spoke. "Last Saturday seemed like a good day to hike to Arch Rock. We walked over to Lashley Lane to pick up our friend, Kristy. We were headed down the street near the park when we saw this cat. She was so cute, we stopped to pet her. When we walked on, she followed us."

"What did the cat look like?" I asked.

"All white, but the hairs were kind of dark at the tips."

In my notebook I scribbled, "Positive ID."

"After a couple of blocks of her padding along right behind us," Beth continued, "we decided to take her with us. Kristy put her in her backpack and gave her a ride. She was so sweet in there and she seemed to really like it."

"We planned to bring her back. We really did." Brittany said. "But, while we were at Arch Rock eating our lunch, the cat disappeared. Like, I mean, she just vanished. We looked for her. Honest. But we couldn't find her anywhere."

"So we came back without her," Beth continued. "We didn't know what house she came from or who she belonged to. So we couldn't tell anyone what had happened. I guess we should have gone around and asked. We didn't. We just hoped she'd find her way home."

Aaron let out an exasperated sigh and shook his head. Dynamike rolled his eyes as if he couldn't believe anyone could be that dumb. I was too annoyed to feel sorry for the girls even when they squirmed a little as I stared at them.

"It's not like we set out to lose the cat on purpose," Brittany said defensively.

"We'd be glad to buy the owner a new cat," Beth offered.

"Sure," Brittany chimed in. "We want to do the right thing."

Clearly they felt bad and wanted to be let off the hook, but I knew it wasn't going to be that simple.

"You don't get it, do you?" I asked. "Mrs. Carabell wants her own cat back, not some other cat. She happens to love the one you guys carted off into the woods and left."

The twins flushed and didn't meet my eyes. I tried hard to get back into my professional investigator role. After all, they had talked with us and told us where the cat was. They could have just lied and pretended not to know anything about it.

"Thanks for the information. We'll try to find the cat. If we don't, we'll remember that you offered to buy a new one." We left the house and held a short meeting outside by our bikes.

"Can you guys pack a lunch and go for a hike to Arch Rock tomorrow?" I asked.

"Sure," said Dynamike.

"Anyone know how to get there?" Aaron asked.

"Not exactly," I admitted.

"Let's stop by the library on our way home," Aaron suggested. "They've got a lot of maps."

At the library, Mrs. Hosler, the librarian, smiled at us. She'd told me once that we were among her best customers. It seemed we always needed to hunt something up.

"Need any help today?" Mrs. Hosler asked.

"No, thanks," Aaron said. "We're just going to look at some maps, and I know where they are in those pull-out drawers in the reference room."

Aaron led the way. Turns out the library had topographic maps of all the city and county parks and trail areas. Aaron knew about them because he and his dad did a lot of hiking. He quickly located the map we needed, and we all leaned over it.

"You know," I said, "I've heard lots of people mention Arch Rock, but I've never actually been there. Good thing you knew about these maps, Aaron."

"Yeah," Dynamike said. "We don't want to get lost ourselves while hunting for a missing cat."

By the time we worked out when and where to meet on Sunday morning and started to head home, a few raindrops were falling. I hoped the rain wouldn't last. It was going to be a long hike to Arch Rock. It was definitely too far to make it there and back before dinner on a school night. If we couldn't go tomorrow, we'd have to wait for next weekend to search for Fortune.

By late that night it was pouring, and in the morning it was still coming down in buckets. Right after breakfast, I made myself a couple of sandwiches to carry on the hike.

"For anything less than a rescue mission I wouldn't let you set out in this, Wink," said Mom as she added a thermos of hot chocolate and an apple to my backpack.

"Aw, Mom," I said, stuffing my sandwiches into my pack. "It'll probably stop pretty soon. And think of that poor cat lost out there."

Dynamike and Aaron arrived together and waited for me on the porch. They were both dripping wet. I groaned inwardly as Mom checked us all out. She made sure I was wearing boots, a coat, my slicker, and a hat.

Bugle stood at my feet, thumping his tail. He looked disappointed when I said, "You can't go with us today, boy," and Mom pulled him back into the house.

"What a day to go out on a case," Aaron moaned.

"A perfect day to find Fortune. It's raining cats and dogs," Dynamike cracked.

Instead of letting up, the rain came down harder and harder. We left the neighborhood streets behind us and started into the park. Aaron had studied the map and said that we could hit the trail that led to Arch Rock on the far side.

We'd all been to this park lots of times. "Let's take the shortcut," I suggested. "It'll save us ten or fifteen minutes."

The regular route was a switchback path that led to a footbridge over the creek. The shortcut meant climbing a steep hill, which was never any fun. Today it was miserable since the path was oozing mud. We slogged through it and then hurried down the hill, planning to cross the creek on rocks like we always did.

"Look how deep the water is," Dynamike said.

It was so deep it was over the top of most of the stepping stones. Aaron, who had long legs and could climb like a mountain goat, was fearless. He barely hesitated. He stepped sure-footed onto the biggest rock near the bank that still stood above the water, estimated where the next rock was under the water, stepped there, and finally onto the last rock. From there he jumped onto the muddy bank. It was so squishy, he almost slipped back in.

I followed, but didn't do quite as well as Aaron. By the ripple going around the second rock, I guessed where it was, but one foot slid off the rock and slipped into water that went up and over my boot. Boy, was that water cold! Somehow I kept my balance and pulled my foot back up, found the next rock, and made it to the muddy bank.

Dynamike stood on the first large rock and hesitated, balancing there. Then he stepped for the second rock, fell short, and went sideways into the creek.

"Mike!" I yelled and reached out toward him. I slid down the slippery bank and almost fell in the water myself.

Dynamike was washed about fifteen feet down the creek. Aaron and I ran along the bank after him.

"Watch your head! Feet first! Grab something," Aaron yelled.

Finally Dynamike reached out and grabbed onto a big boulder near shore.

"Hang on, and don't try to stand up," Aaron shouted.

Dynamike struggled against the water and held on tightly. Aaron grabbed a tree at the bank with one hand and grabbed my hand with the other. I leaned out and could just reach Dynamike's hand. We managed to pull him out. He was sputtering and shivering.

"Are you hurt?" I asked.

"Scraped up a little," he said. "And my left ankle hurts. I twisted it when I fell." Dynamike's teeth began to chatter.

"Can you walk?" Aaron asked.

"I think so."

We helped him up the bank. He was limping and his face was awfully pale. Dynamike and I both stopped and dumped the cold, muddy water out of our boots.

"We'd better get you right home," Aaron said. "You're drenched!"

"If it's all the same to you guys, let's take the long way this time, across the bridge instead of swimming through the water," Dynamike suggested with a crooked grin.

It was slow going. We must have looked like three yellow-slickered musketeers. Dynamike had an arm around each of our shoulders, and together, we helped him limp along. When we got to Dynamike's house, we waited a few minutes while his mother clucked over him and urged him to get right into a tub of hot water.

"Thanks for bringing him home," she said. "I don't think anything's broken—just a few scrapes and bruises. He'll feel better when he's warmed up." Then she took a close look at us.

"You boys better get on home, too, before you catch cold."

We hated to abandon our cat rescue mission, but clearly this was not the day to hike to Arch Rock. We quickly left. As soon as I got home and my mom stopped fussing over me, I peeled off my clothes and took a hot shower. Then I put on dry clothes and came down to the kitchen to eat the lunch from my backpack.

"A little early for lunch, isn't it?" Mom said.

"Yeah, but I'm hungry." The hot chocolate from my thermos tasted good, especially after I shook a lot of miniature marshmallows into it.

As I sat drinking my chocolate, I felt pretty discouraged. The first case for the WHAM Agency had hit a snag. I looked out the window at the pouring rain, thinking about poor Fortune being out there in this.

After lunch, I called Mrs. Carabell and told her what had happened. I didn't have good news to report, but I thought it was important to keep a client informed.

"You brave, brave boys," she said. Her voice sounded as if she were fighting back tears. "Going out in this awful rain and almost getting yourselves drowned."

"We're okay," I reassured her. "But because Arch Rock is so far away, we can't hike there and back on a school day. That means we can't try again until next weekend. I hate to think of Fortune lost out there."

"I'm running an ad in the lost and found section of the newspaper. And I suppose there's always a chance she'll make her way home by herself. If so, I'll call you right away, Wink."

"Okay, and if not, we'll go next Saturday. The WHAM Agency doesn't give up on a case. We'll find your cat," I promised. After I hung up, I sat there for a moment and found myself hoping I would be able to make good on that promise.

It continued to pour all day Sunday. That night, I sat with Mom and Dad watching a flood report on the evening news. You don't often see your own town featured on television, but tonight Santa Rosa was on national TV.

"Look!" I yelled, jumping to my feet. "The Golden Hotel." And sure enough, on the screen was a work crew with a crane struggling to remove some huge, uprooted trees that were dangling in the water along the back of the creek near the old hotel.

Then the screen showed a scene from the opposite side of town. "My gosh! That's Bear Creek," Dad said in disbelief. Normally, Bear Creek was a thin trickle that any kindergartner could hop over. Now it was a raging torrent of roiling, muddy water and fallen trees.

The newscaster was saying that the highway connecting Santa Rosa with Healdsburg had been closed after several cars became stalled in standing lakes of water. Helicopter cameras showed stalled cars and others that had slid off the road.

The next morning when I woke up, I looked out the window. Yuck! The rain was still coming down. I couldn't help thinking of poor Fortune, wet and lost in the woods, and of Mrs. Carabell, who was sick with worry.

Quickly I smoothed my bed, got dressed, and stumbled into the bathroom. I sprinkled water on my face; there was no use overdoing it, as I'd get a good shower on the way to school anyway. Then I brushed my hair. As usual, one piece right in back stuck up so I tried to slick it down again.

"Won't this rain ever stop?" I asked, entering the kitchen and finding two grim faces sipping coffee and listening to the radio. "Hey! What's wrong?"

"Shhhh!" my mother interrupted. "Listen."

An excited newscaster commented, "We've just checked with Superintendent of Schools, Jim Ryan, who has announced that, due to hazardous road conditions, no students will be bussed from the mountain areas to Santa Rosa schools today. However, school will be open for all other students. Stay tuned for more flood news at seven-thirty." The voice stopped, and music began to play.

"No fair!" I complained. "Why do town kids have to go to school while the mountain kids get to stay home?"

"I'm surprised that schools are open at all," Mom said.

Dad and I set the table while she put the griddle on the stove and stirred up some pancake batter.

"I think I'd better drive you to school, Wink," my dad said, switching off the radio. "That way I'll get an early start, too. If Bear Creek floods, I'll have to take some fancy detours to get to campus today."

My Dad taught at the college in Rhonert Park, which is really close to Santa Rosa. Normally it took him twenty minutes to get to work. But this morning was anything but normal.

Fortified by a stack of hot pancakes, I pulled on my raincoat and boots, then ran back to my room to get my math homework. I couldn't find it, even though I vaguely remembered putting it in a safe place. Where?

Dad was waiting for me by the back kitchen door, which led to the garage. He had his old leather briefcase and carried a huge, black umbrella.

"Mom!" I yelled. "Did you see where I put my homework?"

Mom located it right away. It was carefully folded in half and tucked safely in the *TV Guide*. I've never understood how my mom always knows where missing things are. I think it's a special sixth sense she has. I wish I had it, but I don't think it kicks in until you're grown up.

Anyway, I'm sure that with her genes, I'll make a great detective someday.

"The streets are empty. Lots of kids must be sitting tight waiting to see if school's canceled altogether today," Dad said as we drove along.

The gutters were overflowing onto the sidewalks. I saw a tricycle upended at the curb. The big front wheel spun around and made a spectacular waterwheel.

"Be sure you go straight home after school today," Dad warned as he let me out. "Your mother will worry."

Inside school, the halls were almost empty. I went to my homeroom, hung up my raincoat, and tugged off my boots. Then I headed for the library and settled down in the magazine corner. Gradually more kids filtered in. When the bell rang, I hurried to class.

Aaron and Dynamike were there. When they walked over to talk to me I noticed that Dynamike was still limping a little. Half the seats in the classroom were empty.

Allison Parsley came in, bangs dripping wet, looking like a sheepdog. She was one of my least favorite people in Mrs. Tilden's fifth grade class. Allison had a high squeaky voice and was always waving her hand to give answers that were wrong half of the time.

Maybe I wouldn't have minded Allison so much if it weren't for her tagalong little sister, Mary Margaret, who was one of the stubbornest human beings I'd ever met. I'd learned to steer clear of that kid.

Allison walked immediately to the tissue box, grabbed a couple, and dried her glasses. Among other late arrivals was Jo Miller, Allison's best friend. For a girl, Jo wasn't half bad, although I'd never understood her terrible taste in friends. Today her soaked braid looked like an old rope hanging down her back.

It was a long day with no outdoor recesses. Our teacher didn't want to start anything new, because so many kids were absent. So she gave us some free time to work on the research paper she'd assigned last week. We were each to choose a famous person or event to write about. She'd suggested topics like Exciting Earthquakes, Awesome Athletes, Incredible Inventors, or Magnificent Musicians. Aaron probably already had a subject in mind, but I didn't. I was sure Dynamike didn't either. No rush. The paper wasn't due for two weeks.

I browsed in some books, but couldn't concentrate. Every time I looked through the window, I found myself thinking of Fortune out in this miserable weather. I was relieved when the rain stopped around two o'clock. The clouds still looked threatening, but at least the pause in the rain let us walk home from school without drowning. I was really glad, because we went a lot slower than usual. Dynamike didn't complain, but he was limping.

When I got home, Bugle greeted me at the door with wild tail thumping. I pulled off my slicker and boots and put them in the closet. I looked in the kitchen, but I didn't see anyone. Then I heard a funny sound in the basement.

3

I went into the kitchen and heard the noise again. Like something, or someone, being dragged across the basement floor. I felt a prickle of the hairs on the back of my neck.

"Mom?" I yelled down the basement stairs. "Are you down there?"

"Wink? Oh, I'm glad you're home."

It was my mother. I let a sigh of relief escape.

"Come on down. I need some help. And close the door behind you so the darn dog stays up there."

"Uh, oh," I whispered to Bugle, pausing for a moment to scratch the favorite spot behind his left ear. Mom only referred to him as the "darn dog" when he'd done something wrong. "What kind of trouble have you gotten into now? Are we both in the doghouse?" Bugle started to whine when I slipped through the door to the basement and quickly shut it again, leaving him on the other side.

"What's wrong?" I asked, clumping down the stairs.

Near the bottom, I looked around and my mouth fell open. One side of our basement now had a long, narrow lake of water in it. The lake was beneath the windows all along one wall of our unfinished storeroom. Along the edge of this new lake were wet dog prints. I could see why Bugle was banished.

Mom had dragged everything away from that outside wall—an old chest of drawers, a table lamp without a shade, some barbells and weights, a fan we used in summer, and an exercycle that no one had used for months. These things were now all pushed together in a heap in the center of the storeroom.

A wet stain, like a snail trail, showed the route of sopping wet boxes that had been dragged across the storeroom floor. They led to the open door of our finished rec room on the other side of the stairs.

"It looks like a disaster area. What happened?"

"It's all this rain," Mom said. "The lawn couldn't soak up any more water. A big pool collected in a low spot in the backyard by the window well. It seeped into the basement and got a good head start on me before I noticed it."

"Wow!" I said, looking around. "What a mess!"

"I'm dragging the boxes one by one over into the rec room to open them up and see how much damage was done."

"I'll help. What's in all these boxes, anyway?"

"The light ones on top are filled with Christmas tree ornaments. The ones in the middle have camping and fishing gear. And to be honest, I don't know what's in the boxes at the bottom. Maybe old books or magazines."

Mom tugged at another of the heavy boxes. "Ugh," she groaned, as she stood straight and put a hand to the small of her back. I went to help her. Between us, we finally managed to drag all the boxes into the rec room. Mom had already put a plastic drop cloth down on the carpet in there, and we set the boxes on it.

Looking at the pile of boxes, I said, "This is proof that our family never throws anything away that might be useful."

"You're right. What a pile of junk!"

"Yeah," I agreed, "I'm impressed."

I looked out the garden-level windows. "It isn't raining now. Maybe the storm's over. Do you think?" I felt a twinge as I pictured poor Fortune, lost out in this. She must be soaked and miserable.

"I certainly hope so. Now, let's open up these boxes and take whatever's inside out to dry."

Mom opened the flaps on one of the three wet boxes and peered in. "Oh," she sighed in relief. "We're in luck, Wink. There's nothing in here but small carpet scraps. I'm not even sure why I saved them. Out they'll go."

"Hey, don't throw them away," I said, "I might need them." One look at Mom's face made me stop talking. This was not the time to tell her of all the possibilities these carpet scraps opened up, like making a scratching post for a cat or designing a science fair experiment to test different brands of carpet stain removers. Maybe I'd be able to rescue these perfectly good carpet scraps later, but not now.

"Let's see what's in this big light one." She opened a second box. "Oh, good," she said. "Rolled foam pads that we use to put under sleeping bags on camping trips. No harm done. Let's just lay them out flat to dry."

Then Mom headed for the third box. Unlike the other two, this box was tightly tied with twine. And it was big, almost five feet long, I'd guess. First, Mom tried to untie the knot. Then she tried to break the string. Finally she asked, "Would you get me the scissors, Wink?"

I hurried upstairs, making sure Bugle didn't squeeze his way through the door, and hurried back again with the scissors. While she cut the string, I studied the box. It looked liked somebody had planned to mail it. There was an address label glued on top, but the ink had run. I couldn't make out what it said.

Mom pulled away the pieces of string, used the scissors to slit the package tape, and opened the box. "Oh, dear," she gasped as she unfolded a piece of tissue paper. "Look, Wink. It's filled with framed paintings. She began to pick them up one by one by the corners, peeking at each one. The top paintings were fairly small, but the one on the bottom was really big.

"Paintings?" I stared down at them. The really big one was of an ugly, old, falling-down barn. I couldn't draw anything, but Dynamike was a great artist, and I knew he could paint a barn ten times better than this. "What are these doing down here? Are they old pictures you and Dad packed away because you didn't like them anymore?"

"No," Mom answered. She frowned. "I haven't the faintest idea how these pictures got down here. I've never seen them before."

"Well, we'd better take them out." I grabbed the box and pulled it toward me and it came apart in my hands. It was sopping wet. Carefully we lifted each tissue-wrapped canvas painting out of the carton. As Mom unwrapped the next to last one and set it on the drop cloth to dry, I pulled out the really big bottom painting.

"This one's soaked," I said. "I think it was completely under water. Should we wipe it off, do you think?" Without waiting for an answer, I wadded up a piece of the tissue paper and dabbed at the surface of the painting.

"Stop, Wink!" Mom ordered. But she was too late. I could see that the tissue was already stained with green paint.

"Oh, dear. It's ruined," Mom said. "And the worst part is, I don't even know who it belongs to."

I set the painting next to the others. "The rest of them look all right," I said hopefully. "And maybe this one can be fixed." I looked at it again. "I only smeared the paint in the bottom right corner, but I sort of removed a bush."

Mom stood up. "Tonight we'll ask your father to clear up this mystery. He must know how these got here."

I stared at the row of paintings and felt my heart beat a little faster. "I think we may have uncovered another job for the WHAM Agency."

"The what?" Mom asked.

"The WHAM Agency," I repeated. "Stands for Winklehockey, Aaron, and Mike. We're private eyes. You know we're currently investigating the case of Mrs. Carabell's missing cat."

"Oh, yes," Mom said. "Well, what I need right now is a cleaning service, not a detective agency. So how about getting the mop and a bucket? I'll get the space heater, and we'll see if we can get things dried out in the storeroom."

I was in the middle of mopping when the phone rang. I ran upstairs. It was Dynamike.

"I just got back from the clinic," he said. "I'm still limping a little, and you know Mom's a worrywart. She thought we should get X-rays of my foot and ankle."

"And?"

"Everything's fine," he said, "just like I told her. The doctor showed us the X-rays, and they're way cool. Matter of fact, I'm going to do some reading about how X-rays work. I think I may write my school research report on 'Incredible Inventions.' The doc said I should take it easy this week and keep my foot up and ice it when I'm at home. But he said it'll be fine in a couple of days."

"That's great," I said. "I wasn't sure you'd be able to go with Aaron and me this weekend to look for Fortune."

"Wouldn't miss it," he assured me.

"Wink!" Mom called from downstairs. "Come get your dog."

I realized that when I'd run upstairs to answer the phone, I'd left the door open. "Gotta go," I said. "We had a flood in our basement and Bugle is trying to turn a big mess into an even bigger one. I'm glad your foot's okay. Talk to you later."

I ran downstairs. Bugle wore his hangdog expression and Mom looked pretty exasperated. "He's got a nice clean bowl of water upstairs, but does he drink that? No, he prefers drinking dirty water out of your mop bucket."

Poor Bugle. He really did want a snack. I whistled. Bugle followed me back up the steps, and I shut the door on him again. Then I finished cleaning up the storeroom floor.

"Leave everything in the middle of the room," Mom said. "It could rain again."

When Dad got home, we met him at the door. He was flushed and started talking fast, telling us about the accidents he'd seen and about all the detours he'd had to take to get to and from campus. The moment he paused for breath, Mom and I chimed in.

"Carl, the basement flooded," Mom began.

"And we found a big box of paintings down there," I added. "Do you know where they came from? 'Cuz if you don't, we've got a real mystery on our hands. Maybe a case for the WHAM Agency."

"Whoa!" Dad held up both hands. "Slow down, please. Remember my nerves are shot. What's this about a flood? Paintings? What WHAM Agency?"

So Mom went first and described the flood in the basement. Then I filled him in on the box of paintings and explained about the newly formed private investigation agency.

"I'd better go see how bad it is," Dad suggested.

With the space heater going full blast, the storeroom was starting to dry out.

"If there's no more rain for a while, we may be all right," Dad said. "Now, what about this box of paintings."

In the rec room, the dry boxes were stacked in one corner. The foam pads were spread out across one half of the room on a drop cloth. And the paintings were resting in two rows on the other half.

"These four paintings were on top, and I think they're fine," Mom said, indicating one row of pictures. "But the great big one at the bottom got quite wet."

"Hmmmm," Dad said. He looked at the paintings and frowned. "I'm no art expert, but I'd have to say this is a pretty ugly set of pictures. I wouldn't want them hanging upstairs in our house. Where could they have come from?"

"You don't recognize them either?" I asked. I felt a little thrill race through my body. I was getting even more certain that this was a case for WHAM.

"This is the box they were in," Mom explained, picking up the soggy pieces near the door. "There's an address label on top, but the ink is smeared."

I carried the wet empty carton over to the floor lamp and rotated the box trying to catch the light. "I think it says, 'Professor Richard Little.'"

Dad looked blank. "Richard Little. Doesn't sound like anyone we know. Oh, wait. Could it be Professor Richard Knettle?"

Dad took the box from me and squinted at it. "That's it," he said. "Of course! Two summers ago when we went to Canada, we rented our house out during July and August to a visiting professor in the English Department. Remember? That was Knettle."

"Oh, yes. I remember the name," Mom said. "We never actually met him. We left the keys with the Jensens, and Professor Knettle moved in and out again while we were away. Do you suppose these paintings are his?" A stricken look crossed her face. "Oh, I hope they aren't valuable."

"If he paid much for these," I said, "he was robbed."

"I doubt that they're valuable, or he wouldn't have forgotten and left them down here," Dad said. "Besides, you rescued them right away. They're probably all right."

"One of them isn't," I confessed. "I tried to dry it off with tissue paper. And some of the paint came right off."

"Uh, oh," Dad said. "Let me see."

I picked up the huge painting and handed it to him.

"I'm sorry, Dad. I was trying to help. I didn't mean to ruin it."

Dad looked closely at the painting. "I think it's very odd that paint would smear like that."

"If these really do belong to Professor Knettle, and he wants them, perhaps we should take the ruined one to Mr. Matthews, the art dealer downtown," Mom said. "We could see what he has to suggest."

I took the painting back from Dad, held it to the floor lamp, and studied it again, closely this time. "That's weird," I said. "It looks to me like there's another painting underneath where the bush was. I think maybe there are initials or a name in the corner, and it kind of looks like there's a campfire."

4

"Look right here," I said, and Mom moved in closer. "Can't you see something underneath? Down there in the corner where I've rubbed away the paint?"

"I think I do!" Mom leaned in for a closer look.

Dad took the painting then and held it close to the light. "You're right! It does looks like initials, and maybe another picture underneath the top layer of paint."

Clearly this called for action from a WHAM investigator. I had to check this out. I turned and started up the stairs. "Be right back," I called over my shoulder. My heart was pounding as I grabbed some paper towels, got one of them damp, and ran back down again.

I set the painting on the drop cloth, and with the wet towel in one hand and dry ones in the other, I began to gently rub at the smeared corner of the painting.

"Wink, do you think you should do that?" Mom looked worried. "You seem to be making it worse."

"I figure this corner is ruined already. I won't touch any other part." I continued to rub. The surface paint came off pretty easily.

Dad knelt beside me. "This isn't oil paint you're taking off," he said as he felt a corner of the wet, green paper towel and rubbed it between his fingers. I could hear the touch of excitement in his voice. "It's a water-base paint that has been put on to cover up the original oil surface."

"Why would anyone do that?" asked Mom. "Paint over a picture?"

I went back to work on the corner again. Almost all of the bush was off now. I still couldn't quite make out what was underneath; a scrawled name or initials and something rosy. "Wow! It could be the *Mona Lisa.*" I didn't really think it was the *Mona Lisa,* but that was the only famous painting that I knew by name. "Maybe it was stolen. To hide it safely, the thief painted a country barn right over the Mona Lisa's face."

"Oh, Wink," Mom said with a mischievous look. "How strange it hasn't been on the news. Do you suppose that no one has noticed that the *Mona Lisa* is missing from the Louvre? And isn't it odd that the clever international art thief who masterminded this theft hid the painting in our basement and then forgot all about it?"

"Okay, okay," I said, and smiled. "I guess you're right. It's probably not the *Mona Lisa.* But it could be some other famous painting."

"*Mona Lisa* or not," Mom said, "it does seem very strange. And I don't think you should rub on that painting any more. If it is valuable, I don't know what we should be doing, but I'm pretty sure we shouldn't be rubbing it with a damp paper towel."

Just then the doorbell rang. I set the picture down and hurried up the stairs to the front door. There were Aaron and Dynamike.

"Hi, Wink," Aaron said. "Can you come over and play a video game before dinner?"

"Shhhh." I looked up and down the street for any sign of suspicious-looking characters. With what might be a hidden masterpiece downstairs, I couldn't take chances. "Come inside. Quick!"

"What's going on?" asked Dynamike.

"We can't talk outside," I whispered. "Anyone passing by might hear."

"Hear what?" Dynamike wanted to know.

"Come on in," I whispered, "and I'll tell you about it."

Dynamike and Aaron came inside. I closed and locked the front door. "It's just that we can't be too careful," I said.

"The rain leaked into our basement and soaked a lot of boxes. We opened them up to dry. And guess what? One of them is filled with paintings!"

"So, you've got a box of wet paintings in your basement," said Aaron. "Too bad. But what's the big deal?"

"They don't belong to us." I explained. "And one may be a very valuable stolen painting."

"What makes you think that?" asked Aaron.

"You know, you're a skeptic," I said. In our spelling list at school last week, we'd had the word "skeptic." I wasn't sure what it meant, so I looked it up and learned that a skeptic is someone who doubts. At the time, I didn't think I'd ever have a use for that word, but now I did.

"No, I'm not. You're just being overly optimistic," Aaron said, pulling out another word from a recent spelling list. "What makes you think this wet painting is valuable?"

"It's not just a wet painting," I explained. "When I tried to dry it with a piece of tissue paper, some of the paint came right off. My dad thinks someone has deliberately painted over the original. Come see. I think it's a case for the WHAM Agency."

I led the way downstairs into the rec room where Mom and Dad were still bent over the big painting, which they were holding close to the lamp.

"Hello, boys." Mom smiled at Dynamike and Aaron. "I think you're right, Wink. There's definitely another painting underneath. And the way that top paint came off so easily makes me think it was just put on to cover up the other one. But why?"

"Maybe Professor Knettle doesn't even know that one painting hides another," I said. "He may not realize that it's valuable."

"We don't know that either," Dad reminded me. "Just because someone painted one picture over another doesn't mean that the one underneath is a fine work of art."

Mom chuckled. "You're right, Carl. I guess all that talk about the *Mona Lisa* got me thinking that we've got an art treasure here instead of something ready for the trash." She turned toward the stairs. "I'm going to start dinner."

"Would you let Aaron and Dynamike see where the top layer of paint came off?" I asked. No matter what anyone else thought, I wasn't about to abandon my theory that this was a hidden masterpiece and a case for WHAM.

While my Dad held the painting, Dynamike and Aaron stood near the light and stared at it quietly. I could tell by the looks on their faces that they were impressed. I kept staring at what looked like the rosy glow of a campfire and those squiggly initials, burning them into my mind, but I couldn't quite make them out, no matter how hard I tried.

"What are we going to do?" I asked.

"We'll leave the painting here to dry. I'll call Mr. Jensen and try to get Professor Knettle's address or phone number. Then I'll get in touch with him and ask him about the box of paintings."

"Do you think Professor Knettle will be mad when he finds out we've discovered his secret? Do you think he stole some valuable paintings and hid them here? Do you think—"

Dad cut me off. "What I think is that we should wait until I get in touch with Professor Knettle. Then we'll find out what he says about all this."

"This could be big news in the art world," I insisted.

"More likely these paintings have no value at all. Professor Knettle might paint for a hobby. Maybe he painted during the summer he lived here. When he didn't like the first picture, he just painted another over it."

"Do your really believe that, Dad?" I held my breath.

"No," he finally said. "I can't imagine using a water-base paint directly over oils. I don't think that Professor Knettle painted these. It's a real mystery."

I grinned at Aaron and Dynamike. They looked as excited as I felt.

"Isn't there anything we can do while we're waiting to find out where Professor Knettle is?" I said.

"Have you got something in mind?" Dad asked.

"Well, remember I told you we've formed the WHAM Agency? And we're working on our first case, Mrs. Carabell's missing cat. We haven't gotten very far with that, because we have to wait for a weekend to hike all the way to Arch Rock. We can't do that until first thing Saturday. But in the meantime, we could take on the Case of the Hidden Masterpiece."

"Sure we could," Dynamike chimed in.

"Right," Aaron agreed. He didn't sound skeptical any more.

"We need to call in expert help," I continued. "Agencies do that all the time. I mean, private investigators can't be experts in everything. Mom said something about talking to a Mr. Matthews at his art shop in town. Could we take the painting to him? Maybe he could tell us if it's really valuable."

"Hmmm," Dad said. "We can't do that. These paintings probably belong to Professor Knettle. We'd have to ask him before we took one to an art expert and asked how much it's worth."

I watched the bright-eyed enthusiasm disappear from Dynamike's and Aaron's faces. They now looked about as happy as Bugle did after a long "bad dog" scolding. I was discouraged, too. Waiting wasn't something that came easily to me. I was already frustrated in not being able to find Fortune. I'd been hoping for some action.

"As soon as I learn anything, I'll let you know," Dad promised. "In the meantime, can I count on the members of the WHAM Agency to not talk about this?"

We nodded.

>─┤─◆〉─○─〈◆─┤─◄

Every day that week I kept wanting to blurt out to everyone I saw, "There's an art masterpiece in our basement!" But I managed to keep my mouth shut. Dynamike and Aaron did too. We only talked about the painting in whispers as we walked home from school.

We talked about Fortune, too. How was she surviving living out in the wild? I called Mrs. Carabell every afternoon, but she had no news. No one had answered the ad in the paper, and Fortune hadn't come home.

Dad hadn't been able to contact Professor Knettle. Apparently the Jensens were out of town and he had no way of contacting him. It was hard to wait. Two juicy cases waiting for WHAM and nothing happening.

Friday after school, Aaron and Dynamike came over to my house. We sat for a while and talked about our cases. They were as frustrated as I was. Nobody was in the mood to watch TV or play a board game. We all felt restless. But somehow we had to get through the afternoon. In the morning, we'd leave bright and early for Arch Rock.

"How about throwing some passes down at the park?" I finally suggested. I was tired of sitting around looking glum and feeling worried.

I grabbed the scarred, old ball out of the closet in my room and we headed out. Bugle managed to slip through the door, too. His tail, already curled up tight like a watch spring, almost touched his shiny black back. He knew we were headed for the park.

Not far from the park, I caught a glimpse of a white tail as a cat slipped behind a garage. "Hey! Could that be Fortune?" I yelled.

Aaron, Dynamike, and I went racing behind the garage. We found a startled cat with black patches on her body. Discouraged, we trudged back to the sidewalk.

In the park, we took turns throwing long passes near the lake while Bugle happily sniffed at shrubs and trees. Then Bugle set off for the water's edge. No doubt he was planning to chase and terrorize the half-dozen ducks that lived there.

Just as I was fading back to catch a long pass, I heard a familiar, piercing voice. "Mayday! Mayday! Mad dog approaching. Over and out." I let the ball sail by as I searched for the owner of that voice. I knew it was Mary

Margaret. Suddenly she leaped out of the bushes, walkie-talkie in one hand, and caught Bugle by the collar. With her short, spiky hair sticking out in all directions, Mary Margaret looked like a wild cat.

I guessed the call over the walkie-talkie had been meant for her sister, Allison. I quickly looked around, and saw Allison standing about fifty yards around the lake, leaning forward and staring at something in the water.

Bugle struggled frantically and managed to squirm free of Mary Margaret's one-handed grip. He'd fallen into Mary Margaret's clutches a few times in the past and had learned the hard way that if he didn't want to be dressed in her sweater and tucked in a baby buggy, he'd better stay out of her reach. Bugle abandoned his duck hunt and hightailed it back to me for protection.

Allison seemed to be trying to catch a frog. She was reaching out with one hand while holding her walkie-talkie in the other. I watched her step on a large, flat rock. It was too much to hope that she'd fall in.

"It's not fair!" I grumbled, as my friends trotted up. "Just think what we could do with that equipment! Mary Margaret needs a walkie-talkie like a fish needs a bicycle. With a voice like hers, you don't need radio equipment to reach across the lake."

"I wonder where they got them," Aaron said.

Mary Margaret spied us, and I heard her speak into her transmitter. "Allison. Come quick. It's Wink and his friends."

Allison abandoned the frog, or whatever it was she was trying to catch, and hurried over to Mary Margaret. Then they both headed toward us.

"Hi," Allison called. "Aren't these walkie-talkies great?" I took one look at the smirk on her face and decided on total silence. I couldn't trust myself to speak. I was furious with the injustice of it all. Walkie-talkies wasted on these two!

Aaron, on the other hand, spoke smoothly and easily. "Yeah. Where'd you get them?"

"Uncle Ken sent them to me for my birthday," Allison said. "Aren't they cool?"

I continued to say nothing. Bugle and I both kept a close eye on Mary Margaret. She'd sneaked up on me once from behind, jumped on my back pretending to be a saber-toothed tiger, and almost strangled me to death before I got her off. You couldn't take your eyes off that kid. From the ragged look of her bangs, her mother must have momentarily forgotten that lesson and let her get near the scissors.

"Say, how far do your walkie-talkies reach?" Aaron asked.

"Oh, I don't know," Allison answered. "They reach from Mary Margaret's bedroom to mine."

"You haven't actually tested out their limits?" Aaron said.

I wondered why Aaron was wasting our time talking to these two.

"No, why should we?" Allison asked. "We've got better things to do than spend time running dumb experiments on long distance walkie-talkies."

"Of course you do," Aaron agreed smoothly, in his best Monopoly banker's voice. "But it's important information. Everyone who sees them will want to know. The farther they reach, the more valuable they are."

"Really?" Allison said.

"Tell you what, if you and Mary Margaret loan them to us for a day, we'll run some tests for you and report exactly what their capabilities really are, in writing," Aaron offered.

Wow! I thought. So that's what he's up to! You've got to hand it to this guy. Never misses an opportunity. But I knew he would never talk Allison Parsley into anything.

Just as I thought, Allison was not convinced. "Oh, no you don't, Aaron Bates. You're not going to walk off with our walkie-talkies for a day. Not unless we get something in exchange."

"Yeah!" Mary Margaret chimed in. "What do we get?"

"What you get is information," answered Aaron. "Free. You're looking at the members of the WHAM Agency. Normally we charge a fee for the private investigation work we do for clients. But we'll test your equipment at no charge. We'll even push aside some of our other pressing business to complete the tests tomorrow."

I saw a big smile break out across Dynamike's face. He'd finally figured out what Aaron was up to. But I knew it was hopeless. Allison would never fall for this.

"You supply us with the walkie-talkies first thing tomorrow morning, and we'll return them with detailed written information by five. And of course, we'll give you our standard contract stating that the equipment will be in our careful hands for the day and will be returned promptly and in excellent condition."

That Aaron. He came up with ideas as fast as I got mosquito bites on a summer night. He made it sound as if we really were doing the girls a favor.

"Would the contract be typewritten, dated, and signed?" demanded Allison. She was no dummy when it came to TV lawyer talk.

"Of course," Aaron agreed. "And it's free," he stressed.

An interesting look crossed Allison's face. "All right," she said. "It's a deal. Shake." She stuck out her grimy-looking hand.

Aaron didn't flinch. He shook it solemnly. "Deal."

I could hardly believe he'd pulled this off. It had been too easy.

The girls went back to the edge of the lake, and the three of us left the park with Bugle trotting at our heels.

"Good work!" Dynamike whispered when we were out of earshot.

"I can't believe it." I said.

Aaron looked pretty pleased with himself. "I thought that went pretty well."

"You're a genius," Dynamike said. "They'll be great to use on our hike to Arch Rock to hunt for Fortune."

"Right," I said. But I felt a little uneasy. I was remembering the crafty look on Allison's face when she shook hands. Were we going to regret this? Dynamike and Aaron hadn't had as much experience as I had with Allison. What did she have in mind? She'd agreed too easily. And I knew that any time Mary Margaret was involved, it always spelled trouble with a capital "T."

I hurried into the kitchen Saturday morning and found Mom and Dad already there having coffee. Mom said, "You're up early. Off on your hike today?"

"Yeah, finally!" I glanced out the window at a bright sunny morning. "And this time it isn't raining." I poured myself a glass of milk and got out a bowl and cereal. I'd need my energy today. "Allison and Mary Margaret are loaning the WHAM Agency their walkie-talkies. We'll test them while we're out looking for Mrs. Carabell's cat. They'll be great for keeping in touch."

Thinking about keeping in touch made me wonder about Professor Knettle and the mysterious paintings. "Dad, do you think Professor Knettle will call today?"

Dad lowered his newspaper to answer me. "No, Wink. I'm not sure he's even received my letter yet. Once he does, he may phone or write, but he might just wait until he's in town to pick up his box of paintings."

I had overheard Dad talking on the phone with Mr. Jensen on Wednesday night and knew that Professor Knettle would be stopping by to visit the Jensens in a couple of weeks. Mr. Jensen gave Dad the professor's

Oregon address, but suggested that rather than mail the box, it might be easiest to wait and hand-deliver the paintings.

I hated the idea of waiting, but no one else seemed to be in any hurry. Everyone had completely lost sight of the fact that we might have a hidden masterpiece in our basement.

Mom said, "If the WHAM Agency is on a search-and-rescue mission in the woods today, maybe I should pack a big lunch for my private investigator. Would you like that?"

"Thanks, Mom. Your sandwiches always taste better than mine. And could I have some lemonade for the canteen? It looks like it's going to be warm today."

"Sure. You mix up the lemonade and add lots of ice." She got up from the table and set to work on sandwiches.

While she did that, I checked my supplies. My Swiss Army knife was in my pocket. I had rope, matches, first aid kit, a power bar, and a rain poncho in my pack. Aaron said he'd be bringing a flashlight, so I didn't need that.

"Here's a can of tuna to slip in your backpack, too, in case you find the cat. The poor thing will be starving. And wear your hiking boots," Mom added. "Sunny or not, it might still be pretty soggy up in the woods after all that rain we had."

"Okay," I said. I wondered if all the big private eyes like Sherlock Holmes and Sam Spade had mothers who worried about wet feet.

At ten to eight, Dynamike and Aaron came over. I put on my backpack, heavy with lunch and supplies, and we headed toward Raven's Roost, our tree house on Mrs. Carabell's vacant lot where we always went to make plans and talk. We'd agreed to meet Allison and Mary Margaret there. Bugle trotted along with us and sat at the foot of the tree when we climbed to our perch.

A few minutes later, the girls arrived carrying their walkie-talkies. They hadn't backed out of their half of our agreement. "Hi," Allison called.

I scrambled down. When I reached the bottom, Allison handed over her walkie-talkie with a little smile. I tried my best not to look suspicious, but I still wondered what she was up to. It simply wasn't like Allison to be agreeable.

"Aren't you going to invite us up?" Mary Margaret demanded, one hand on her hip and the other tightly clutching her walkie-talkie to her chest.

"Nope," I replied. The last thing on earth I wanted was girls up in Raven's Roost.

Especially these two girls.

"But I want to climb up and look." Mary Margaret hugged her walkie-talkie with both hands.

By this time, Dynamike and Aaron had climbed down, too.

"Oh, let her climb," Aaron said. "Otherwise we'll be standing here all morning."

"Hand it over first," I demanded and held out my hand.

Mary Margaret gave up the precious walkie-talkie and then quickly climbed the boards nailed to the tree trunk like a ladder. When she reached the top, she shaded her eyes with her hand and looked in all directions.

"Land ho!" she suddenly bellowed in a voice loud enough to be heard in the next county. Apparently she was pretending to be high in the sails of a ship.

"Okay, the ship's safely anchored, so come back down," I ordered. I felt silly playing along with her, but experience had taught me, you did it Mary Margaret's way, or no way. I was actually kind of surprised when she did what I asked. I was afraid I might have to pretend to be a pirate and carry her down kicking and screaming.

"Where's the agreement?" Allison demanded.

Aaron took a folded sheet of paper out of his pocket. He'd printed it on his dad's computer, and all three of us had signed it. It looked very official. "Here you are."

Allison read the document carefully. Satisfied, she turned to leave, saying, "Be sure you take good care of our equipment." The two girls turned and started to walk back down the street.

"Let's get going," I said, and we headed out with Bugle at our heels. I would rather have waited until I was sure that Allison and Mary Margaret were far away from Raven's Roost, but we didn't have time to waste. We had a long hike ahead of us.

Soon we were at the entrance to the park. A sign pointed the way to Arch Rock. Aaron pulled something out of his backpack and entered the details of where we were.

"What's that?" Dynamike asked.

"It doesn't look like a compass," I said, looking at the object in his hand.

"It's a GPS 4000," Aaron said. "My dad uses it all the time. If we were to get lost, it'd show us how to get right back to this spot."

"Gosh," I said. "With walkie-talkies to keep in touch and a GPS to show the way, the WHAM Agency has gotten pretty high tech."

"Yeah," Dynamike said. "Whatever happened to a trail of bread crumbs?"

Today we took no shortcuts. We couldn't risk another near drowning and river rescue attempt. In the shady areas it was still muddy from the rain, but out in the open the ground was already dry.

In just over an hour, Dynamike suggested we stop under a big tree and eat.

"You mean right now?" It amazes me that anyone as little as Dynamike can, at any moment, put away a ton of food. I think he must carry some mutant piranha genes somewhere in his body.

"Could there be a better time? Dynamike asked.

"It's another two or three hours until we get to Arch Rock," Aaron said. "Let's wait until we're there."

Dynamike sighed, but he didn't argue. We continued up and over the ridge.

As we hiked through the woods we tested the radios, and I recorded the results in my notebook. We checked out hills and ravines, and paced off distances. These walkie-talkies were really powerful. We would have liked to do some treetop to treetop testing, too, but didn't dare waste any time. Poor Fortune had been lost long enough. All the while we walked, we kept our eyes open for any sign of the cat.

We finally reached Arch Rock just after twelve. We threw ourselves to the ground. All of us were tired and more than ready for lunch. Mom had packed peanut butter and jelly sandwiches, a banana, and a heap of chocolate chip cookies.

I tossed my bread crusts to Bugle. He caught them in midair and never missed once. Feeling generous, I gave him a broken cookie, too. I washed everything down with cold lemonade from my canteen.

Rested and full, I could now concentrate full-time on worrying, and I was a champion worrier. Where was that cat? Would we find her? Was Fortune even still alive?

"Time to search," I said.

We decided to split up to cover more ground and search the nearby area, hoping Fortune had remained near where she was dropped off. We agreed to meet back at Arch Rock in half an hour. Aaron took a walkie-talkie, made another reading with his GPS, and started up the hill. Dynamike headed off to the left on his own.

I walked to the right, walkie-talkie in hand. "Here, kitty, kitty. Here, kitty, kitty," I called every now and then. It made me feel silly. Bugle listened to me, cocked his head to one side, and looked puzzled. Then he put his nose to the ground and ran ahead. Had he picked up a scent? He certainly chased plenty of cats out of our yard.

Every now and then, my walkie-talkie crackled. "See anything?" Aaron asked.

"Negative," I replied. Our biggest excitement was when I spotted a crow and when Aaron said he was watching a squirrel. I was getting desperate for some sign of the cat. Our very first case, and we were getting nowhere. Then Aaron called and said, "Time to head back to the rock." My heart sank.

When we were all back together, feeling discouraged because none of us had seen any sign of Fortune, I said, "Fortune's been gone more than a week now. I guess we should have known she wouldn't be sitting here by the rock waiting for someone to come get her."

"Yeah. She could be hiding out of sight or may have wandered off in any direction," Aaron said.

"You're right," Dynamike agreed.

Maybe the cat was nowhere near here. Some hiker may have found her and taken her home to another town. But I kept my discouraging thought to myself. "So now we have to take the time for a real good look around. We've got to find her." I was thinking how awful it would be to have to report our failure to Mrs. Carabell. "Let's search for a another hour and meet back here."

"Right," Dynamike agreed, "and it's my turn to have one of the walkie-talkies." Aaron handed his over.

"We'll synchronize our watches," I said. "It's one-thirty. Let's meet back here at two-thirty so we can make it back home by five. This time, I'll go up the hill. Dynamike, you go right. Aaron, you go left."

I walked a long way and was about ready to admit defeat and head back, when I noticed a dark spot against a cliff. It was partway up a brush filled and fairly steep hill. Curious, I decided to go for a closer look. Bugle suddenly began to sniff and look very interested.

I could finally make out that it was a small cave up in the rocks. Bugle ran on ahead of me, his nose to the ground. "What is it, boy?" I asked. "What can you smell?" I picked up on his excitement and felt a little thrill go down my spine. Was he actually on the trail of something? Could it be Fortune?

Bugle scrambled up the rocky ledge to the opening of the cave. Then he stopped stiff in his tracks. When I got close, I could hear a strange, hissing sound. It seemed to be coming from the cave. Fortune? Snakes? Cautiously, I approached, pulled Bugle aside, and standing on the ledge just below the cave, peered in. The hissing had stopped.

It was dark back in the cave, and I couldn't see anything. I wished I had my flashlight with me. I spoke into the walkie-talkie. "Dynamike? Do you read me?"

"I copy you. What's up?" Dynamike asked.

"I may have found something, and I don't want to leave here. If it is the cat, I don't want her to sneak away. Find Aaron, and as soon as you can, both of you head up the hill."

"I can see Aaron. He's heading back," Dynamike said. "We'll be there as quick as we can. When you spot us, radio directions to where you are."

"Roger. Over and out."

They must have hustled, because it didn't take long for me to spy them from my perch high on the side of the hill. I used the walkie-talkie to guide them right to me.

When they reached me, Aaron took out his flashlight and shone a beam of light into the cave. The three of us crowded close together on the ledge trying to see. Way in the back, I could make out what looked like a bundle of white fluff.

"Fortune?" I yelled. Could it be? My heart was pounding.

"Here, kitty, kitty," Aaron cried.

"Give me a hand," Dynamike said. "I'm not tall enough to see in there." I cupped my hands and gave him a boost up. "I can see something white," Dynamike said, "but it's not moving."

Bugle began to bark in excitement and the hissing started up again. Whatever was back in that cave didn't like dogs, that was for sure.

I let Dynamike down on the ledge again and pulled the rope out of my pack and fastened it to Bugle's collar. Quickly, I walked partway down the hill and tied him to the nearest small pine tree a few yards away. He whined as I climbed back up to the ledge below the cave.

I pulled out my Swiss Army knife and rummaged in my backpack again for the can of tuna. Good old Mom! Quickly I opened the can. "Here, kitty, kitty," I coaxed.

The smell of the warm tuna was strong. I reached into the mouth of the cave and set the can down at one side of the cave opening.

A meow rewarded me, and then a bedraggled white cat with burrs in her coat crept out of the recesses of the cave toward me. I tipped out the tuna onto the rock and the three of us kept very still. It was Fortune! We'd found her. I looked at my buddies and saw the same joy and relief in their eyes that I was feeling.

Greedily Fortune began to eat the food. I directed the flashlight beam into the recesses of the cave and could just make out something white wiggling far in the back. I heard a soft mewing.

"Well," I whispered to Fortune who gulped the tuna. "It's no mystery why you didn't try to find your way back home. You've been busy taking care of a new family, haven't you?"

While Fortune ate, Aaron and Dynamike boosted me up onto the ledge so that I could wiggle on my stomach back into the cave. It smelled musty and damp and wasn't high enough for me to stand. As I inched forward, I tried hard not to think of spiders, but my skin was crawling.

About six feet in, I found three white kittens, their eyes closed, mewing softly. I gathered them carefully into the crook of one arm and backed out on my stomach.

At the mouth of the cave, I handed them down to Aaron and Dynamike. Then I gently took Fortune in one arm and slid over the lip of the cave and back to

the ledge. Fortune snuggled against me, and I heard a little purr.

"Let's make a nest for them," Dynamike suggested. He handed his kitten to Aaron and quickly took off the sweatshirt he had tied around his waist. He wadded it up and stuffed it into my backpack.

"Okay," I said, putting Fortune down onto the sweatshirt. "Now put the kittens around her. Be real careful. We don't want them to get squashed."

Fortune mewed anxiously until all three kittens were nestled near her. Then I loosely tied the flap of the big pocket, being sure there was plenty of space for air. Aaron held the pack as I carefully put my arms through the straps and lifted the wiggling bundle. Dynamike untied Bugle, and we triumphantly started back down the trail.

We hiked homeward at a fast clip, stopping every now and then to peek in and check on Fortune and her kittens. As we went, I whistled. The WHAM Agency had solved its first case. I couldn't wait to deliver Fortune to Mrs. Carabell! Energized by our success, we made good time hiking back home.

Since we would walk right past Allison's house on our way to Mrs. Carabell's, we decided to return the walkie-talkies and my scribbled notes to Allison and Mary Margaret first.

As we approached their house, I whispered, "Let's not tell the girls anything about the kittens or we'll never get away from here."

Aaron stepped forward and rang the bell. Over the noise of the TV from inside the house, we heard Allison and Mary Margaret running to the door. With a twinge of regret, I watched Aaron and Dynamike hand over the walkie-talkies. I reached into my back pocket and took out my notes. "Here's your report," I said, handing it over.

One of the kittens took this moment to meow.

"What was that?" asked Mary Margaret.

"What?" Dynamike asked innocently.

"I heard a cat," Mary Margaret said.

"Must have been the TV," Aaron said. "Hey, thanks for letting us test out the equipment. They're great walkie-talkies." He actually reached out and shook hands with Allison before turning and walking down the steps.

Bugle, Dynamike, and I hastily followed him and hurried to Mrs. Carabell's. I told Bugle to sit, took off my backpack, and rang the bell.

When Mrs. Carabell saw the three of us standing on her doorstep, I knew that the looks on our faces immediately told her that we'd been successful.

"You found her, didn't you?" she finally managed to say. "You found Fortune!"

We nodded and stepped inside the house.

"My stars!" Mrs. Carabell exclaimed, peering inside as I took off and opened up the backpack containing Fortune and the three kittens. "Thank you, thank you!" There were tears in her eyes and for a long moment she didn't speak.

Finally she carried the backpack over to her chair and gently set it down. Then she picked up Fortune in one arm, sat down, and cradled the cat in her lap. One by one, I lifted the kittens from the pack and set them in Mrs. Carabell's lap.

As Fortune began to purr, Mrs. Carabell beamed. For a moment, Fortune and the kittens had all her attention. Then Mrs. Carabell seemed to remember the three of us standing there. She reached over to the end table beside her chair and picked up a small box with her free hand.

She handed it to me, saying, "I wasn't sure you'd find Fortune, but I knew how hard you'd try. And after you risked your lives in that creek last week, I went to the printer to get these. I've had them right here waiting for you. When word gets out about how good you are, you're going to have a ton of business."

Inside the box were white business cards with the words WHAM Private Investigation Agency in bright red. Beneath, printed in black, were our three names, Carlton "Wink" Winklehockey, Aaron Bates, and Michael "Dynamike" Murphy. Our telephone numbers were printed under our names.

"Wow!" I said. "Do these ever look official! Thanks a million, Mrs. Carabell."

"It's the least I could do," she said. "You returned a Fortune to me!"

We each took a card out of the box and stared at it.

"It's a perfect reward." Aaron ran his fingers over the raised printing.

"Cool," Dynamike said.

"Thank you, Mrs. Carabell," I said, stowing the box in my backpack.

We left her bustling about making a bed for the kittens in the kitchen. Then we climbed back up to Raven's Roost, which was right next door in the vacant lot. I looked around anxiously and was relieved to find everything as we'd left it. A breeze was blowing, and it felt cool and peaceful high in our tree.

"Who would have guessed that Fortune would stay up in the mountains all that time waiting for us to come to the rescue?" said Dynamike.

"Quite elementary, if you ask me," said Aaron, in his best Sherlock Holmes voice. "What else could she do with three kittens? With all that rain, drinking water was no problem. And she must have hunted mice and bugs up there in the woods to live on. I'll bet she would have found her way home again when the kittens were big enough to travel."

"Maybe," I agreed. "She's one smart cat. But I'm sure glad she's home now. Mrs. Carabell was worried sick."

"Speaking of that," said Aaron, "we'd better get on home. I'll call up the Patterson twins and tell them we found Fortune. They were feeling pretty guilty."

I pulled the business card out of my pocket. "I'm going to hang onto this one. You know how some people frame the first dollar bill they make in a new business and hang it up in their office? Well, I'm going to frame this."

"Case number one, The Missing Cat, solved!" Dynamike said.

From my back pocket, I pulled out my stubby pencil and my spiral notebook and printed SOLVED at the bottom of the page.

As we clambered down the tree, I said, "I hope everybody is ready for case number two, because the Case of the Hidden Masterpiece is waiting."

6

"Case number two? What case? Are you talking about those old paintings you found in your basement?" asked Aaron. "You really think those ugly pictures are master-pieces?"

"Of course not. Not the pictures you see on top," I said. "But there could be hidden masterpieces under-neath. Why else would anyone paint over them?"

"I don't see any real mystery." Dynamike looked down, avoiding my eyes. He and I usually agreed on things, and I could tell he was uncomfortable siding with Aaron on this. "Your dad seems pretty positive those paintings belong to that professor guy and that he might have painted them. The only question is, why did he leave them in your basement?"

"Why?" I repeated. I paused for dramatic effect. So far, this was not going as I had hoped. My buddies couldn't seem to see an exciting case for the WHAM Agency even when it was right in front of their noses. "That's the mystery we have to solve." I tapped my spiral notebook with my stubby pencil. "Was the professor hid-ing these valuable masterpieces out of sight until things cooled off so he could sell them on the art black market?"

"I wish we knew whether or not they were valuable," Aaron said. "If they're worthless, and I think they are, it doesn't really matter how they got in your basement or who painted over what."

Like a balloon that had just sprung a leak, I felt the excitement of a few minutes ago drain away. Although all I'd had a chance to do so far on this case was hurry up and wait, I was intrigued by those old paintings. The thought that they might be worth nothing was really deflating.

"If only we could take one of the paintings to an art expert and get his opinion," I grumbled. "But my dad says no. He says we've got to have Professor Knettle's permission before we do anything. I think we're wasting a lot of time."

"Speaking of time," Aaron interrupted, looking at his watch. "We'd better be getting home. If I'm late to dinner, I'll be in big trouble."

We scrambled down the tree to where tired old Bugle was waiting. He was pretty pooped from our hike to Arch Rock. Bugle gamely struggled back to his feet, tail wagging weakly, and followed us. I was tired, too, and worried about our next case, but I was proud of having done a good day's work. We might not have made any progress on the hidden masterpieces, but Fortune and her kittens were home.

Over the next few days, since we were now successful private investigators, with one solved case and a satisfied customer behind us, we handed out our new business cards. We offered them to everyone—the principal, the secretaries, the custodian, and all our teachers. But we were offered no new cases. School continued in the same old routine.

I did spend one evening on the Internet. I went to Google and typed in "missing masterpieces." There was plenty of interesting stuff to read, like stories about paintings missing from collections because they had been destroyed by floods and earthquakes. I learned that a famous painter named Vincent van Gogh had a brother, Theo, who simply gave away a lot of valuable paintings to those who came to the artist's funeral.

But I wasn't interested in paintings that had been destroyed or given away, I wanted to know about those that had been stolen and hidden away. There were a few of these, and that gave me a glimmer of hope. But most of these thefts had occurred years ago, and I had no way of connecting them with the hidden masterpieces in my basement. So, reluctantly, I gave up my search and hunkered down to wait for Professor Knettle to arrive.

Now and then we popped in on Mrs. Carabell and looked at the kittens. Their eyes had opened, and they could climb out of their basket. Mrs. Carabell had named them Treasure, Precious, and Boodle. She was always scooping up one or another from some kind of mischief, but she never complained. Mrs. Carabell was

71

one happy lady. And Fortune was one pampered mama cat enjoying all kinds of special tidbits.

It was the Monday before Thanksgiving when a letter finally came from Professor Knettle. As soon as Dad tore open the envelope and began to read it to himself, I asked, "What does it say?"

"Not much," Dad replied, handing over the short note. "He just says he'll be spending Thanksgiving with the Jensens and not to bother mailing the pictures to him because he'll come over here to collect his paintings then."

So the paintings really did belong to Professor Knettle. I read and re-read the letter, thinking that I might uncover some clue between the lines. But I didn't. There was no hint of stolen art treasures and no explanation of what the paintings were doing in our basement, either. Just a thanks for finding them and a promise to come over to collect them. No big deal at all.

"If you don't mind, I'll keep this," I said, holding up the letter. "You know, part of my case files."

"Fine." My dad didn't smile, but I thought I saw the corner of his mouth twitch. I don't think he took the WHAM Agency very seriously.

I put the letter and envelope in my pocket, intending to store them in my room. "Are you just going to hand those masterpieces over to him?" I asked.

"Now, Wink," Dad said. "Remember we don't know that they're masterpieces at all. I'm certainly going to ask some questions, and I'm sure he'll tell us about them, but we may never learn the secret of those paintings."

"What do you mean, we'll never learn the secret?" I asked, alarmed.

"When Professor Knettle comes, we'll have to give him back the paintings. They're not ours. He'll be perfectly free to take them and leave. He doesn't have to explain anything to us."

"He'd better explain! Because if he doesn't, I think the WHAM Agency will need to call in the FBI."

Dad said, "Why don't we wait and see."

I hate it when grown-ups say that. But since there was no choice, that's exactly what I did. This year, I was going to be the most thankful person in Santa Rosa when Thanksgiving finally came around!

>—+—◆>——○——<◆>—+—<

Our teacher, Mrs. Tilden, told us that we could do a play for the winter holidays. Rather than settle for a well-known Christmas story, our class decided to write its own. I realized it had to be appropriate for the holidays, but I was still hoping for a mystery, something like "Who Stole the Presents?" or "The Case of the Missing Fruitcake."

Allison waved her hand like mad and got to chair the script-writing committee, so naturally Aaron, Dynamike, and I didn't volunteer to be on it. What would be the point? She would ignore all our ideas, and Jo, her best friend, would be on her side. Allison promised the class a super spectacular script that would be ready for casting the following Monday.

73

As Dynamike, Aaron, and I dashed out the door on Wednesday afternoon, more than ready to start our four-day Thanksgiving holiday, I reminded them, "Professor Knettle arrives in town tonight."

"Do you really think he's an art thief?" Dynamike asked. This time he looked me in the eye, and I knew that he wanted me to be right.

"I don't know," I said. "But I sure think there's something funny going on. I'll call you as soon as I find out anything."

I hadn't been home more than ten minutes before the telephone rang. Mom answered it. In case the call was from Professor Knettle, I hung out near her, pretending to be looking for something in the fridge.

"Hello? ... Yes, this is Mrs. Winklehockey. ... Oh, yes, Professor Knettle. We've been expecting to hear from you."

I closed the door of the refrigerator and stopped pretending. "Ask him about the pictures," I whispered.

Mom held up a palm to shush me and continued.

"I'm sorry, my husband isn't home right now, but I know he's eager to see you. Could you come over this evening, say around seven or eight o'clock? ... Good. That would be fine. We'll see you then. Thanks for calling."

Mom hung up the phone and looked at me. "Seven-thirty tonight," she said.

I looked at my watch. "That's four hours to wait."

"Well, after all this time, I'm sure you'll be able to hold on a little longer, Wink. Frankly, I'll be glad when this whole matter is cleared up. Come on. Help me set the table for dinner. We'll eat early and get things cleaned up before our company arrives."

After dinner that night, Dad called a meeting. Although Dad called it a family conference, I knew that it was being held for my benefit.

"Professor Knettle will be here in half an hour," he began, as if Mom or I could possibly have forgotten that. "When he arrives, we've got to be careful about the way we act and what we say. I'm afraid we may have let our imaginations run wild."

I felt my face flush. Dad had said "we," but we all knew that he thought I was the one who'd let my imagination run wild.

"You're right." Mom reached over and squeezed my hand.

"Wink," Dad continued, "you seem to believe that Professor Knettle is part of an international art smuggling ring. We have no reason at all to suspect that. As far as we know, he's a perfectly ordinary teacher. Just like me."

"No way," I insisted. I was outnumbered, but I wasn't going to give up easily. "You don't hide one picture by painting another over it, and you don't hide boxes of paintings in other people's basements."

"Professor Knettle may have painted these pictures," Dad went on. "He may give us an explanation as to why one picture was painted over another. Or he may know nothing about that. Let's try to take it easy tonight and not get too excited."

Mom nodded in agreement. "You're right, Carl. Wink has almost convinced me that these are masterpieces."

"But Dad," I protested, feeling a sense of panic. "What if he takes the paintings, says thank you very much, and leaves without telling us anything?"

"Once we point out the spot where the top layer came off and show him there's another painting underneath," Dad said, "he'll have to say something, won't he?"

"I hope so," I said. And under my breath, I added, "He'd better."

Mom made a fresh pot of coffee, then we all sat down to wait. When the doorbell finally rang, I jumped up and yelled, "I'll get it."

I opened the front door. I'd imagined he'd be dressed in a black suit, wearing shiny black shoes, and stroking a long, drooping mustache. Wrong! I hated to admit it, even to myself, but he looked like an ordinary guy, a little older than my dad, maybe, with sandy hair and wearing a blue sweater. I invited Professor Knettle into the living room. He introduced himself, sat down, and Mom quickly poured him a cup of coffee. I sat down, too, and kept quiet even though I had about a million questions wanting to fly out of my mouth like bats out of Carlsbad Caverns.

Professor Knettle was the first to bring up the subject of the paintings. "I really owe you an apology. I didn't intend to store that box of old pictures in your basement all this time. I'm afraid it's been in your way."

"Not at all," Mom assured him. "If the basement hadn't flooded during a big rainstorm, we probably wouldn't have come across your paintings for several more years. We have so much junk stored down there we didn't even notice your box."

"But we are worried," I broke in. "One of your pictures may have been water damaged. Your box was at the bottom of a pile and got really wet. I ruined a corner of one painting by dabbing at it and trying to dry it. Some paint came off, and that's when I noticed that there seems to be another picture underneath."

"Well, you don't need to worry about ruining the painting," Professor Knettle said. "Those paintings are of no value whatsoever."

In the silence that followed, Mom and Dad and I exchanged quick looks.

"No value?" I said, not believing my ears. I swallowed hard.

"None at all."

I reached for my back pocket, but stopped myself before I pulled out my stubby pencil and spiral notebook. I knew it wouldn't be polite to take notes during a social visit. I'd just have to try to remember everything. In my most professional voice I asked, "How can you be sure they aren't valuable?"

Mom shot me a look, but I put on my innocent expression and smiled at our guest.

"I bought them when I was staying here two summers ago," Professor Knettle said. "At that time, an old house up on Pine Street was being torn down. Prior to wrecking it, they offered all kinds of things from the house at a public sale."

"Up on Pine Street?" I said, encouragingly.

"Yes. Apparently the owners, a Judge Winters and his wife, were well-known residents. The judge died a long time ago. Then when his wife died, she left the house and land to the city. She hoped they'd use it for a small local museum or library."

"Gee, I don't know of any building like that up on Pine Street," I said.

"Soon after the sale, I read in the paper that the old place was torn down," Professor Knettle went on. "The city decided it was in such bad shape, it couldn't be saved, but the land was valuable. They hoped to eventually build a branch library on that spot and name it after the Winters family."

"That's right," Mom chimed in. "I remember reading something about it later that fall. They tore down the house, drew up plans for a Winters Local History Library, and even put the foundation in. That's as far as it got before they ran out of money. I think they still plan to build when more funds are available."

"And you say you went to a sale there?" I prodded. If looks could kill, my mom would be guilty of murdering her only son.

"Yes," Professor Knettle went on. "There were lots of valuable antiques in the house. The city council decided to sell them and put the money into the building fund."

As Professor Knettle talked, I watched him closely. Was he telling an elaborate story he'd concocted, or was he telling us the truth?

"My wife collects antiques," Professor Knettle said, "and her birthday's in July. Since I wasn't going to be home for her birthday, I tried to find a nice antique at the Winters's house to ship to her for a surprise."

Everything sounded logical when Professor Knettle talked. He was a cool customer, all right.

"If those old pictures were antiques you bought for your wife's birthday," I interrupted, "why didn't you mail them to her?" Aha! I'd tripped him up.

Mom shot me another look. But my question didn't seem to bother Professor Knettle. He said, "I sent her something else."

"You bought her these pictures and then didn't send them to her?" I asked. I think I sounded like a TV lawyer questioning a witness he didn't believe.

"Well, you see, after I got to the sale, I realized I didn't know much about antiques," Professor Knettle explained. "The prices were high, it would cost quite a bit to pack and ship an antique, and I didn't want to spend a lot of money on something my wife might not like."

"Very sensible," my mother said.

"But since I was there, I wandered around," Professor Knettle continued, "and checked the bargain section in the backyard. It was mostly junk that had been stored in the basement. That's where the box of pictures was. Frankly, I thought the paintings were ugly, but the old oak frames looked good to me. They were cheap—twenty-five dollars for the whole box. So I bought them. When I got home, I slapped a label on the box. I was going to mail it, but then I thought I'd just take it home with me at the end of summer. I stuck it in your basement."

"And then forgot all about it," Dad said. "I can see how that might happen."

"I bought a different gift and sent it to my wife. By the time I got around to packing up to drive back home in August, that box of old pictures had completely slipped my mind. I never thought of it again until I got your note."

I had to admit to myself that his story sounded pretty logical. He seemed sincere. How could I face Aaron and Dynamike and tell them the professor wasn't an art thief after all?

"Wink, why don't you and I go and get the paintings," Dad suggested. "We can show Professor Knettle the corner where there seems to be another picture underneath."

I didn't need a second invitation. We went down to the basement. I carried the four smaller paintings, while Dad carried the big one.

"I'm especially interested in seeing the one that's been painted over," Professor Knettle said. "That does seem odd to me."

Carefully, we placed the big painting on the floor right in front of Professor Knettle and I kept a close eye on him. I had to admit, he didn't look the least bit worried. Just curious.

I showed Professor Knettle the place where I had rubbed away the top layer of paint.

"Hmmm," Professor Knettle said. "There's no doubt about it. There certainly is another picture underneath. It looks like a short name or initials and something orange there in the corner."

"What do you make of it?" my dad asked.

"I don't know what to think," Professor Knettle replied. He looked at me, smiling. "Any ideas?"

I'd been waiting for this moment. "Yes," I said, and I pulled out my spiral notebook and my stubby pencil.

7

"I do have a few ideas," I announced in my most business-like manner. I dared not glance at my parents. I knew they were probably shooting me dagger looks. Instead, I flipped open my notebook and pulled out one of the WHAM Agency cards that I kept stashed there. I handed it to Professor Knettle.

"The WHAM Agency is at your service. This is just the kind of case we solve. Now of course, these are your paintings and you can certainly do whatever you want with them." I looked at Dad to be sure he'd heard me say that. "But I think this calls for a little investigating, don't you?"

"Well, yes, of course." Professor Knettle studied my card and looked a little puzzled. "Especially since there seems to be another painting underneath. Very strange. But what should we do?"

"The first thing we need to do is to consult an art expert." I looked Professor Knettle straight in the eye. "And my mother happens to know of a good one, don't you, Mom?"

"Well, yes," Mom said. "There's an art dealer in town by the name of Matthews. He's lived here in Santa Rosa all his life. He sells pictures for local artists, restores paintings, does framing, all that sort of thing."

"He's just what we need for this case," I said. "Would you like to contact him and get his opinion?"

"Sounds like a great idea," Professor Knettle agreed. He gave me a big smile. "I'm willing to invest a few dollars to solve this mystery."

I turned to look at Dad. "Taking the painting in to Mr. Matthews is what I wanted to do two weeks ago," I reminded him.

"It's true that Wink has been anxious to take the paintings to Mr. Matthews," Dad admitted, "but we didn't know how you'd feel about all this. And I thought perhaps you might be the artist yourself."

"Well, I'm happy to say that it wasn't me who painted that ugly picture," Professor Knettle said.

He said this with so much feeling, that we all laughed, and I found myself beginning to really like the professor.

"I'd like to see what's underneath," he went on. "And, of course, I'm wondering about the other paintings, too."

"Why don't we take them all in to Mr. Matthews and see what he thinks and get a price estimate," Mom suggested. "Then you can decide if you want the expense of having him clean them."

"Since Wink has an investigating agency, and since you know the art dealer, Mrs. Winklehockey, would you two mind taking the paintings in?" Professor Knettle asked. "You know, if an out-of-town stranger came walking in with these, Mr. Matthews might think they're stolen masterpieces and that I'm an art thief." He chuckled as if he'd made a good joke.

I squirmed a little. It was true that for days I had thought Professor Knettle might be a crook. I saw my dad trying to hold back a smile.

"We'd be glad to take them in," Mom said. Then she added, "Oh, dear. Tomorrow's Thanksgiving. Nothing will be open."

More complications and delays, I thought. This waiting was going to be the death of me. "How long will you be in town?" I asked Professor Knettle.

"Till Sunday."

"Mr. Matthews's shop may be closed all Thanksgiving weekend," Mom pointed out.

"Well, if it is, I'll have to phone you from Oregon next week to get the results." Professor Knettle stood and thanked Mom for the coffee. He wished us luck, and then Dad showed him to the door.

After the professor left, I looked down at the open box of paintings. "How about that?" I said to my parents. "He doesn't know any more about these paintings than we do."

"Now at least we know where they came from and how they got here," Dad said.

"And it was such a simple explanation," Mom added. "Professor Knettle seems like a nice person. Here we were thinking he might be an art thief."

I reddened again. Mom was being kind, but I knew it was only me who was dumb enough to suspect him of being a thief.

"He is nice," I admitted. "But I still think we've got a hidden masterpiece on our hands. Couldn't we call Mr. Matthews tonight and ask him to come over and take a quick peek?"

"No, we could not," Dad said firmly. "The night before a holiday? Anyway, there's probably nothing underneath except another ugly painting. It can wait until his shop is open."

I could tell from Dad's tone of voice that there was no use arguing. But I didn't agree with him. I wasn't good at locating lost homework, but I had a sixth sense that let me smell a mystery a mile away, and I was positive that something more than another ugly painting was waiting to be uncovered. I just wished I didn't have to wait again.

The next morning I tried to keep busy and keep my mind off the mystery by helping in the kitchen. I peeled the potatoes. I was good at that. And after Mom got out a special tablecloth, I set the table using our best dishes and silver. Sometimes we traveled to be with family for Thanksgiving, and sometimes our relatives came to see us. But this year was a quiet one. Mom had invited another couple from Dad's college, and that was it. So by early evening, company had gone, everything was cleaned up, and I was comfortably stuffed. I found myself with time on my hands.

I went in to the living room where Mom was looking through a magazine. I started speculating about the possible masterpieces we had in our house. She sighed and put down her magazine. "Wink, I don't want to hear another word about those pictures right now. Why don't you find something to do? Go read a book or play a computer game."

She must be kind of desperate. Mom didn't often suggest that I play video games. I went to my room and turned on my computer. But instead of playing a game, I decided to do a computer card catalog search of the public library to see if they had some art books I might want to study. Of course the library was also closed for the holiday, but I could make a check-out list to use when it was open.

I logged on and typed in the word "paintings." Hmmm. Not too helpful. They had over 2,000 books on that topic. Next I tried "oil paintings," because I was pretty sure the hidden picture had been done in oils. This time there were no matches at all.

I decided I must be going about this all wrong. I thought hard. Maybe the way to search was by the painter's name. If only I could read that squiggle that was on the canvas of the picture where I'd rubbed away the green bush. What was the name of a famous painter? The first one I could think of was Leonardo da Vinci. I typed that in and this time there was a listing of 142 books. That was more like it. Did I know of another painter? Yeah, van Gogh. They'd made a movie about him. I typed in van Gogh and two listings came up. One was a catalog of an exhibition of his masterpieces! Wow! What if a van Gogh masterpiece had been stored in our basement?

I sighed. At the moment I had no idea who had painted that picture. And until I did, there wasn't much sense in locating a lot of art books. I'd have to wait. And waiting was my least favorite activity. I went to bed early, but it was hard to sleep. Brightly colored swirls of paint kept whirling through my head.

Friday morning as I bounded into the kitchen, dressed and ready for anything the day might bring, I asked, "When can we go to the art shop?"

"I'm sure it isn't open this early," Mom said.

"I'll look for an ad in the yellow pages," I said. "Maybe it will give the store hours." I grabbed the phone book and quickly found an ad. "It's open from ten to six, daily except Sundays and holidays," I announced.

"The day after Thanksgiving might well be considered a holiday," Mom said. "Why don't you write down the number, and after ten o'clock you can call and see if Mr. Matthews is in today."

"Okay." I jotted down the number. I was feeling lucky. He just had to be open today. "Can Dynamike and Aaron come with us? This is official agency business, after all. The guys won't want to miss out."

"Of course," Mom said, "but explain that you'll phone the shop after ten to see if Mr. Matthews is in, and then you'll call back and let them know."

I called Dynamike and Aaron, and then gobbled down some cereal. At exactly one minute after ten, I called the shop. Mr. Matthews was in and would be happy to talk to us. "All right!" I yelled after I hung up the phone. "The shop's open!"

By a quarter after ten, Mom, Aaron, Dynamike and I were in the car headed downtown. Mr. Matthews's shop wasn't in the new mall, but in the heart of the old downtown area on Main Street. Mom parked the car and opened the trunk. I lifted out the big painting. Dynamike and Aaron carried the box with the other four paintings in it. When we got close, I could see an "Open" sign in the window.

Mom led the way. A small bell jangled as the door opened. Just inside was a short counter with a cash register. Art materials filled the left side of the store: paint brushes, canvas, stretcher frames, tubes of oil paint, watercolor sets, pastels, and charcoal. Along the right side were framing materials.

I sniffed. So many strange smells. I could only identify two of them—paint and turpentine.

On the back wall, paintings hung for sale. A doorway in the rear, half-hidden by a drape, led into a back room. From this room stepped Mr. Matthews.

"Good morning, Mrs. Winklehockey," he called. "And one of you boys must be Wink. I've been expecting you."

Mr. Matthews had lots of white hair, a bristly upper mustache, and wire-framed glasses.

"Hello, Mr. Matthews. This is my son, Wink, who phoned earlier, and two of his friends, Aaron and Mike. Wink has quite a story to tell."

I stepped forward and whipped out our business card, which Mr. Matthews took and read carefully. Then I explained about the flooded basement, the box of paintings, the smeared paint in one corner, and how Professor Knettle told us the pictures used to belong to Judge Winters.

Mr. Matthews said, "And you're wondering if the painting underneath is of any value and whether the water damaged it?"

"Right. One painting hidden under another seems pretty strange."

"Strange indeed." Mr. Matthews smiled. "So the WHAM Agency has an art mystery on its hands, hmm?"

"This isn't our first case," I boasted, thinking happily of Fortune and her kittens, "but it is our first case involving fine art."

"If it is fine art," Aaron interjected.

"And what does Professor Knettle think about all this?" Mr. Matthews asked.

"He's as curious as we are," explained Mom. "I told him about you. He agreed that we should bring them in. If you think it's worth cleaning them, we will. No one cares if this ugly top picture is ruined since he only

bought it for the frame. But we do wonder what's underneath. Do you think you could take a look for us?"

"How could I refuse?" Mr. Matthews smiled and spread his hands. "I love a mystery. And I'd be pleased to be of service to the WHAM Agency." He tucked our card into his shirt pocket. "Let's look at the big one first," he said, pointing to the package that I'd set on the ground.

"Yes," I said, as I reverently handed it over. As soon as it left my hand, I felt a surge of relief and satisfaction that it was finally in the hands of an expert.

Mr. Matthews set it down gently and used a big scissors to cut the string holding the paper with which Mom had covered it. Then he unwrapped it slowly, stood in front of it, and stared.

I stared, too, and I think I stopped breathing.

"Hmm," Mr. Matthews said. "It's a nice old frame. Needs some refinishing, but it could be handsome. I can see why Professor Knettle bought it." We watched him as he ran his hands along the frame. Then he turned the painting over, held the back of the canvas close to his face, and studied the way it had been stretched and attached. "Hmm," he said again, feeling it along the edges. "Yes."

He turned the picture over again and stared at the whole painting. "Muddy colors. Balance is all wrong." He shook his head. Then he peered intently at the corner where I had dabbed off the paint. "The picture on top doesn't have much to recommend it. But you're quite right. There's definitely another painting underneath. Looks like a signature and something orange. Maybe a campfire."

My breath came out in a whoosh! I gave a grin and a thumbs up sign to Dynamike and Aaron.

"Of course, whether the picture underneath is better or worse than the one on top remains to be seen," Mr. Matthews added.

"Oh, come on," Dynamike burst out. "It couldn't be any uglier."

Mr. Matthews chuckled.

"Now let me see the others." One by one he examined them. "Nothing unusual about these at all. They haven't been painted over. No mystery here, and I don't think they're worth much."

"Will you be able to take the top paint off the big one?" Aaron asked.

"Yes," Mr. Matthews said. "There's white gesso beneath the paint, and I don't think it will be too hard to remove. But it will take some time. You see, I can't use rainwater and tissue paper. If the painting underneath is valuable, I must be sure not to ruin it while removing the top layer of paint. It's a good day's work, and I already have a couple of framing jobs that I promised to finish up today."

Mom said, "I'm wondering how expensive this will be. I'm not sure how much Professor Knettle is willing to pay. Can you give me an estimate?"

I frowned, and as I looked over at my buddies, I saw Aaron wince and Dynamike's shoulders sag.

Mr. Matthews smiled. "I'm as curious as everyone else, Mrs. Winklehockey." He put his hand on my shoulder in a friendly fashion. "I doubt if Wink and his friends in the WHAM Agency would get much sleep if we didn't solve this mystery."

"It's been on my mind a lot," I admitted.

Mr. Matthews paused, staring at the painting. His eyes were riveted to the exposed corner. "Tell you what, I'll work on it tomorrow. I was going to be sitting in front of my TV and this will be a lot more interesting."

"Great!" I said.

"I'll only charge for the cleaning materials that I use. I'll toss in my time for free as a donation to the WHAM Agency and to satisfy my own curiosity. It seems strange that Judge Winters would own a picture like this. I knew the judge, and he had a good eye for fine things."

"It's not like it came from their living room," my mom said, being perfectly honest with him. "It was down in their basement."

"Still, it's an interesting puzzle, isn't it?" Mr. Matthews said. "A job that I think deserves special delivery. I have your address here on your business card, Wink. Suppose I stop by tomorrow evening around seven and bring the cleaned painting and the others back to you. Would that be convenient?"

"Fantastic!" I said. Dynamike, Aaron, and I exchanged high fives.

"Professor Knettle will still be here tomorrow night," I said. "Mom, can we invite him over so we can all find out at once?"

"Of course," she agreed.

"I haven't had anything this interesting to work on in a long time," Mr. Matthews said. "But don't get your hopes too high," he cautioned. "We may end up with another ugly painting. Good-bye, now. I'll see you tomorrow night." He shook hands with each member of the WHAM Agency before we left.

As we climbed back into the car, I said, "I feel a lot better now that our masterpiece is in good hands."

"Mr. Matthews is a nice guy," Aaron observed.

"And just think," Dynamike said, "he even knew Judge Winters."

"We'd better hurry home and tell your father how things stand," Mom said. "He's trying not to let on, but he's just as curious as we are. Wink, you can call Professor Knettle and let him know. And Aaron and Mike, of course we're expecting you tomorrow night, too. Everyone in the WHAM Agency will want to hear the news firsthand."

I looked at my watch. Almost eleven. I did some quick mental math. Only thirty-two more hours to wait.

8

I woke up real early Saturday morning, and the hours crept by about as fast as a tired snail. At nine a.m. on the dot, which was the earliest I was allowed to phone anyone on weekends, I called Aaron and then Dynamike. "We've got places to go and things to do," I announced. "Come over as fast as you can."

When they arrived, I took them down to the rec room for a WHAM Agency conference. "I've got a couple of ideas," I said, "on how we might solve this mystery."

"Like what?" Aaron asked.

"First, we've got to go to the Winters's old neighborhood and interview neighbors."

"Why?" asked Dynamike.

"We want to know if either the judge or Mrs. Winters painted," I said. "Or if others who lived or worked in their house might be artists. Maybe one of them painted that ugly barn over that old picture."

"I suppose it's possible," Aaron said, but I could tell from his tone of voice that he didn't think it was very likely.

"What's the second thing?" asked Dynamike. At least he was trying to be encouraging.

"Even though I can't quite read it, I'm sure the picture is signed with some scrawled initials. Maybe we can look at art books in the library and recognize the way that artist signs paintings."

"There are going to be tons of art books," Aaron said. "We'd never find it."

"It won't be easy," I admitted. "But I don't think we need to look at all the art books. There's a campfire in the bottom corner of the picture. I'm pretty sure of it. So I thought we could start with western art. I checked the computer and there are only a few books on painters of the American West. Let's start there."

"Okay," Dynamike agreed. I could tell he was as eager to get going and try to do something as I was.

We both looked at Aaron.

"I think you're crazy. Recognize fuzzy initials? Hunt for a campfire?" He shook his head and sighed. "But okay. If you guys want to go on a wild-goose chase, I'll go with you. What do we do first?"

"Head to Pine Street and check out the judge's neighbors," I said.

We set off on our bikes, zipped across town, and stopped first at the site of the Winters's home. I hadn't paid much attention to this part of town; in fact, I seldom biked out this way. As we'd been told, the mansion had been torn down. The yard was cleaned up, and there were foundations showing where the historical library would be if and when the city ever built the thing.

"So this is where Judge Winters lived," Dynamike said. I could tell from the awed tone of voice and the look on his face that he was impressed. I knew there was no doubt in Dynamike's mind that the judge was a very important man who was so wealthy he kept paintings worth tens of thousands of dollars casually tossed in a box in his basement.

"Yeah." I gave the empty lot a quick glance before heading off again. I didn't want to stand around gawking at nothing. I wanted to do something. We parked our bikes at the far edge of the lot.

"Let's check out the neighbors," I said.

We walked up to a beautiful old house with a manicured lawn and garden and rang the bell. No answering footsteps. I rang again and waited. No one home—or else they were still in bed. The same thing happened at the next two houses.

"Maybe it was a mistake to come on a Saturday morning," I said as we trudged on. "People are either sleeping late or already out for the weekend."

The next place was a small white house that had been converted to offices. It had a sign out front hanging between two posts, which read "J. Orin Perkins, Accountant." I pulled out my notebook and my stubby pencil and scribbled down the name and address, in case it might come in handy.

"He's probably not open on Saturday," Dynamike pointed out, but I walked up and rang the bell anyway. To our surprise, a slightly balding older man answered the door. He smoothed down a few strands of hair and tugged his cardigan sweater into place. Clearly he hadn't been expecting company.

"Good morning," he said. "May I help you?"

"Mr. Perkins?" I asked.

"Yes," he said. "I'm Orin Perkins."

I handed him our WHAM Agency card. "I'm glad you're in. We're wondering if you could answer a few questions for us." I used my best investigative voice. "We're interested in the Winters family that used to live down on the corner."

Mr. Perkins read our card and then looked at us with a puzzled expression. "Investigators?" he asked. "Well, I'm afraid I can't help you. I only moved in here about six months ago."

"Oh," I said, disappointed. "So you never met Judge or Mrs. Winters?"

"No, sorry," he said, and started to close the door.

Aaron piped up. "Do you know which neighbors have lived here a long time and might have known the Winters family?"

Way to go, Aaron, I thought. Wild-goose chase or not, my think-on-his-feet partner was giving it his best try.

Mr. Perkins pointed across the street to an old gray house with lots of white gingerbread trim on it. "Mrs.

Beaufort lives in that house over there. I think she's been a fixture in the neighborhood for years and years. You might try her."

"Thank you," I said, backing off the porch even as I spoke. I was anxious to cross the street and find someone who had actually known Judge and Mrs. Winters.

We trotted over to the gingerbread house. It reminded me a little of the cottage in Hansel and Gretel, and I wondered if the door would be opened by a witch. There was a heavy brass knocker on it, shaped like a lion's head, with a ring through its nose. I knocked and we waited. I knocked again. Drat! At this point I'd even be happy to see a witch. We were really striking out.

"Look," Dynamike said. He pointed out a little brass key in the middle of the door. "I think if you twist this around, it rings." He grabbed the key and gave it a couple of twists. We could hear a loud ringing inside followed by quick footsteps.

The door opened just a crack. "Yes? What is it?" a high, quivery voice asked.

I pulled out another of our cards and handed it to her through the partially open door. "Ma'am, are you Mrs. Beaufort?"

"A little louder, please," she said.

"Are you Mrs. Beaufort?" I repeated, speaking loudly.

"Yes, I am." She opened the door a little wider. I could see that she didn't wear a long pointy hat or even have a wart on her nose. In fact, she was a pleasant looking, white-haired, little old lady with a powdery smell.

Holding our card in a small, blue-veined hand, she studied it carefully. "You know, I've heard of you boys." She broke into a smile. "Which one of you is Carlton Winklehockey?"

I almost fell over in surprise, and I blushed at hearing my full name spoken out loud like that. "That's me," I said, "but everyone calls me Wink."

"And are you Aaron or Michael?" she asked, looking at Dynamike.

"Dyn-uh, I mean, Michael," he answered, reddening as he spoke.

"That makes you Aaron," she said, smiling at him.

"That's right, ma'am," he said.

"My dear friend from the garden club, Mrs. Carabell, talks about you boys and your investigating agency all the time. She told me you rescued her Persian cat."

"Yes, ma'am." I looked at the others and puffed up a little bit. We were famous.

"How could I help you boys today?" Mrs. Beaufort opened the door wide and beamed at us like old friends.

"Your neighbor across the street, Mr. Perkins, sent us here."

"Oh," she said, "Mr. Perkins seems like a nice man, but I don't know him very well, I'm afraid. He's new to the neighborhood."

"Actually, that's why he sent us to you," Aaron explained. "We were asking him about Judge and Mrs.

Winters, and he said he'd moved in so recently he never knew them. He suggested you might, since you've lived here for a while."

"Certainly," Mrs. Beaufort said. "I've lived in this house for more than forty years. Enid Winters was a dear friend. Won't you come in?" She led the way into a little parlor.

Although I'd never set foot in this house before, somehow it seemed very familiar to me. There were the same spindly-legged chairs and those little crocheted pieces on the backs and arms of all the furniture like those at Mrs. Carabell's house.

"Now do sit down. What was it you wanted to ask? Oh, and please speak up, my dears. I'm a little hard of hearing."

I pulled my notebook and pencil from my pocket. As simply as I could and as loudly as I dared, I told her about the box of paintings that had been bought at the estate sale and how one picture had been painted over.

"We were curious about those paintings and wondered if Mrs. Winters was a painter," Dynamike said when I was finished. "We thought she might be the one who painted over the old oil painting."

"Oh, my, no. I shouldn't think so," Mrs. Beaufort said. "Enid was no artist, but she enjoyed displaying the pictures that the judge collected. It was always a joy to go over to her house for a cup of tea." Her eyes misted as she spoke. "It's been a long time now, but I still miss her."

"Did she have a cook or housekeeper living with her?" I asked, trying to take the focus off any sad memories.

"No, Enid took care of that house herself, although it was a big one."

"I've heard it was a great old mansion," Aaron said. "I wish I'd taken a better look at it before it was torn down."

"It was a lovely home," Mrs. Beaufort said with a sigh. "And their rose gardens were the pride of the neighborhood. Folks would drive by and stop just to admire them."

Inspiration struck. "Did they have a gardener?" I asked.

Mrs. Beaufort laughed. "I wouldn't quite call Tommy Farland a gardener," she said. "But after the judge died, Enid hired him to help in the yard. And I have to admit, that young man learned fast and worked hard. Tommy's a good boy, lives just down the block. He worked there all through high school."

"Does he paint?" Dynamike asked.

"I don't know," Mrs. Beaufort confessed.

"Where's Tommy now?" I asked.

"He's in college," Mrs. Beaufort said. "Went all the way up to Oregon State University."

My heart sank. A good lead, and it turned out he didn't even live in California any more.

I slowly closed my notebook and rose. Aaron and Dynamike stood, too. "Thank you for your help, Mrs. Beaufort. If you'll tell us which house it is, we'll walk down and see if Mrs. Farland is at home and whether she'll give us Tommy's phone number and address. We'd sure like to talk with him."

Mrs. Beaufort got to her feet. "Well, you may be in luck. I saw Lucy Farland the other day, and she told me Tommy would be home for Thanksgiving. You just may find him in."

Following Mrs. Beaufort's directions, we hurried down the street to the Farland's house. I was feeling anxious. Thanksgiving was over. Would he still be home? Had we gotten this close only to miss him? Was he boarding a plane right now to return to Oregon?

The Farland house was a lot newer looking than Mrs. Beaufort's and had an ordinary doorbell. I pushed it, listened to the chimes inside, jammed my hand in my pocket, and crossed my fingers.

The door opened and there stood a kid in an OSU T-shirt, jeans, and wire-rimmed glasses with tousled blonde hair. "Are you Tommy Farland?" I blurted out.

"Yeah." He hesitated and looked us over. I think he was wondering if we were selling magazines or something.

I handed him our card. "Mrs. Beaufort from up the street sent us here. We have a couple of questions about Judge and Mrs. Winters, and she said that you used to look after their rose garden."

On hearing Mrs. Beaufort's name, Tommy Farland's face broke into a wide, welcoming smile. "I sure did," he said. "Have a seat," he suggested, pointing to the porch swing. He perched himself on a porch railing as we sat.

"So what do you want to know about Mrs. Winters?"

More quickly and less loudly than my earlier account, I retold the tale of the box of paintings. When

I got to the part about one picture being painted on top of another, Tommy's face flushed. I paused.

"Okay," he said, looking down at our agency card and laughing. "I confess. You guys have found your man. I did the painting of the old barn. Pretty awful, wasn't it?"

"You painted the barn?" Aaron asked.

"Yeah, I'd gone to a county fair with my girlfriend. We went on some carnival rides, and we looked at pies and cakes and animals. In the craft barn, she was oohing and aahing over some paintings, and I bragged that I could do a lot better than that. You know, I just wanted to impress her. I thought I could dash off a painting and wow her with it. Of course, I quickly found out how wrong I was. I had no talent whatsoever, but you don't turn a guy in to the feds for painting an ugly barn, do you?" He grinned.

"It's not so much what you painted, as what you painted over," I explained. "That old canvas you were practicing on happens to have been a very old painting. It might even be valuable."

Tommy Farland's smile disappeared, and he turned pale. As a matter of fact, he looked positively ill. "I can't believe it," he moaned. "You mean I actually painted my bungled barn right over a valuable picture?"

"Right," Dynamike said.

Tommy Farland looked so sad that I added, "At least it may be valuable. We don't really know yet. Mr. Matthews, the art dealer in town, is looking at it today."

"Did I ruin it?"

"We won't know until Mr. Matthews reports back to us," I said. "but I don't think so. He thought he'd be able to clean it up again."

"How did you come to paint over it?" Aaron asked.

"I knew Mrs. Winters real well. She loved her roses, and she was glad to have help in that garden. When I'd go there to work, she'd invite me in afterwards for lemonade and cookies. We'd talk. I think she was lonely after the judge died. One day right after that county fair I told her that I was going to take up painting. She didn't say much then, but the next time I came, she said she had a present for me."

"What was it?" Aaron asked.

"Paints," he answered. "She'd gone right out and bought me paints and brushes. She was like that—always doing nice things for people. She said maybe I'd like to study art when I went off to college. She told me there was a box of old paintings down in the basement that she never wanted to see again, and I could use them for canvases."

"That's funny," I said. "I wonder why she never wanted to see those old paintings again?"

Tommy smiled. "You know, I asked her that very question. She told me that Judge Winters had bought them from a little antique shop up in the Sierra Nevada foothills when they were off on one of their many car trips. That same night, he had a stroke and died. I guess those pictures reminded her of his death. Anyway, she'd put them in the basement. She said I could go right ahead and practice painting over the old canvases."

"Why did you only paint over one?" Dynamike asked.

Tommy laughed. "One was enough. I brought the box of pictures home, and I sat down and painted the bungled barn on the biggest canvas in the box. When I was finished, I looked at it and realized I'd painted the ugliest, crookedest barn that ever there was." He paused. "Did you guys see it?"

"Yeah," Dynamike answered.

"Am I right?" he asked.

We looked at each other, and then all three of us burst out laughing. Tommy joined in. "You're right," I said. "It was one ugly barn."

"Well, I didn't want to hurt Mrs. Winters's feelings, so I didn't tell her about my failure. The next time I went to work, I took the box of paintings back and stored them in the basement. I never mentioned my art ambitions to her again."

"Do you remember what the picture looked like before you painted over it?" I asked.

Tommy frowned. "I really can't remember. It was a long time ago. I think maybe it was a night campfire scene, but I'm not sure."

I gave my buddies a look of triumph. We stood.

"So, if you're not majoring in art, what are you studying at college?" Aaron asked.

"Landscape architecture," he said. "I'm actually pretty good at it. Mrs. Winters would have liked that, I think."

Before we left, he gave us his address, which I scribbled in my notebook. I promised to send him a postcard when I knew more about the picture.

I guess we walked back down the street to our bikes, but I really don't remember. I was floating and feeling great. One part of the mystery was solved. The painter of the bungled barn was Tommy Farland.

We biked home, and Mom fixed us some sandwiches and brought out a plate of cookies.

"Okay," I said as soon as I swallowed the last bite of a chocolate chip cookie and washed it down with a glass of milk. "Let's head out for the library."

Aaron said, "But, Wink. We don't know what we're looking for."

"You're probably right," Dynamike said. "But you never know what you might find until you try. Come on."

9

The moment we entered the library, I went straight to the computer catalog and typed in "Painters of the American West." I wrote down the call numbers of several books, all in the 700s adult section of the library.

Even though our library didn't have a ton of books on Painters of the American West, they had enough so that I could tell we'd never be able to browse through them all in an afternoon. I hoped maybe we'd get lucky.

In the 700s section, we poked around and each grabbed a book. Aaron sat down with *The American West: Painters from Catlin to Russell.* And just before I could reach up and snatch it, Dynamike snagged *Masterpieces of the American West.* That title sounded really promising, because I was still sure our painting was a masterpiece. I took *Painter of the American West, Albert Bierstadt.*

We sat at a big old table and turned pages. Art books are thick. Aaron was flipping pages and looking impatient. Dynamike, who loved art, seemed to be enjoying

himself. And, as I looked through my book, I got more and more intrigued.

"We're getting nowhere." Aaron closed his book with a snap.

"I'm not so sure about that," I said.

"Did you find something?" Dynamike closed his own book and eagerly leaned over to look at mine.

"Not exactly," I admitted. "But this Bierstadt guy did a lot of painting in California up in the Sierra Nevadas."

"So?" said Aaron.

"So, Judge Winters bought the paintings on a trip up in the Sierra Nevadas. Remember? That's what Mrs. Winters told Tommy. And this book says that sometimes he used his initials instead of signing Bierstadt. I'm pretty sure our painting has initials on it. This book doesn't show all of Bierstadt's paintings, but it does have a list of them by name. One is called *Campfire in Yosemite,* and one is called *Around the Campfire.* I'd sure like to see those two, because I believe there's a campfire in the corner of our hidden picture."

"Where could we look for those paintings?" asked Dynamike.

"How about the Internet?" suggested Aaron.

We put the art books back on the shelf and went to one of the library computers that was connected to the Internet. I used Google and typed in "Bierstadt Yosemite." Several sites came up, and we clicked on one. It had views of Bierstadt's Yosemite paintings. They were beautiful, but none of them had a campfire in the bottom right corner.

Then I typed in "Bierstadt - Around the Campfire." Again, lots of sites came up. I clicked on one, and a small painting appeared on the computer screen. The moment I saw it, I caught my breath. The image was tiny, only about two by three inches, but there was definitely a campfire in the bottom right-hand side of the painting.

I looked at Dynamike and Aaron and grinned.

"Hey! Just because there's a campfire in the corner, that might not mean anything," Aaron reminded me.

"But then again, it might!" Dynamike insisted.

"Make it bigger," Aaron said, and although he'd been pooh-poohing my find, I could hear the excitement in his voice. I clicked on the image, enlarging it.

We all leaned in, quietly staring.

"Could that be it?" Dynamike finally asked.

"Hey, look!" Aaron pointed at the screen. "Right there. Beneath the picture. It gives the dimensions of the actual painting. That'll help." As he read them out loud, I wrote the numbers down in my spiral notebook. "It's 24 by 50 inches."

My mouth fell open. I hadn't measured it of course, but I knew the painting in our basement was about four feet long. Could it be? Was it possible? Had we found an old Bierstadt?

After everything we'd learned that morning, when I got home, I couldn't stop talking about Tommy Farland, Albert Bierstadt, western art, and our masterpiece. My parents were happy to find out who had painted the bungled barn, but they weren't so impressed with my library research. Like Aaron, they thought I had no real foundation for my hopes, and no real proof that our painting was *Around the Campfire*. Still, in my bones I felt sure I was right.

At supper, Dad suggested that we not talk about the painting even though it was on all our minds. I tried not to, I really did. But right in the middle of Mom and Dad's discussion of some important vote in Congress, I blurted out, "What'll we do if the painting really is a valuable Bierstadt?"

Dad sighed before he said, "That's for Professor Knettle to decide."

"Let's worry about that if and when it happens," Mom suggested. "Now, how about some ice cream for dessert?" At least if you had to change the subject, ice cream was a good way to do it.

At a quarter to seven, Aaron and Dynamike arrived. I took them up to my room. Bugle tagged along. We alternated between talking about the painting and running to the window to check out cars that were driving by to see if any belonged to Mr. Matthews or Professor Knettle.

It was about five minutes to seven when a station wagon finally turned into our driveway. I went tearing downstairs. Dynamike, Aaron, and Bugle were right behind me.

"This is it!" I shouted, racing for the door. I flung it open just as Mr. Matthews was raising his arm to ring the bell.

He pulled back, startled, and then laughed. "That's what I call a quick response. Do you detectives have an electronic eye on this door?"

"Come in, Mr. Matthews," said Mom, who had reached the door and was standing right behind me.

Mr. Matthews carried the big painting, which was wrapped in brown paper and tied with string. He set it gently against the wall. "Be right back," he said, as he left again and went back out to the car to bring in the box of other paintings.

"Let me take your coat," Mom offered when he returned.

Just then, Professor Knettle drove up. He quickly parked and joined us by the front door and Mom made the introductions.

"Let's all sit down in here," Dad suggested, leading the way into the living room.

Mr. Matthews picked up the big painting while Professor Knettle followed with the box of smaller paintings. I studied Mr. Matthews's face for a clue. What had he learned? Shouldn't a good detective be able to tell? I was about to explode with curiosity.

"May I offer you a cup of coffee?" Mom asked.

"Thank you," Professor Knettle said.

"I'd enjoy that," Mr. Matthews agreed.

Inwardly, I sighed. This would take another few minutes. The "groans," as I called all grown-ups when they gathered in groups of four or more, took their time at making small talk and getting comfortable. I stared impatiently at the brown package leaning against the side of the sofa, but I kept quiet.

Then, as if there'd been some invisible signal, everyone stopped talking at the same moment. Mr. Matthews looked at me. I think he could read faces better than I could. Maybe he could tell I was about to burst. He cleared his throat slightly and began to speak.

"When I first saw this mysterious painting, I wasn't sure what to think. But since it came out of Judge Winters's home, even though it was only in his basement, I realized it was worth a look. The judge owned many valuable pieces of art.

"So I worked slowly and carefully to remove the top painting of a poorly executed barn and landscape. I started in the same corner where Wink first blotted it with tissue. Beneath that layer of paint, sure enough, I found an old oil painting."

"I knew there was a masterpiece underneath," I said. "I knew it!" I looked triumphantly around the circle of faces.

"I didn't hear him say anything about a masterpiece," Aaron whispered.

"It has to be," I insisted.

"If you two would be quiet," Dynamike growled, "maybe we'd learn what Mr. Matthews found."

I shot a glance at my buddy who'd been fidgeting in his seat and realized he was as anxious as I was to know about the picture.

"Well, let me tell you at once that, though it isn't in perfect condition, and it's not the *Mona Lisa,* I believe you do have a work of art of considerable value."

"Yes!" I shouted, jumping to my feet and pumping my arms in the air. "Yes!"

Carefully, Mr. Matthews undid the knots of string, pulled the paper aside, and placed the painting on the carpet with its back propped against the couch. Each of us moved to get a good view.

One look was enough. Aaron, Dynamike, and I exchanged glances. "It's a Bierstadt!" I said. *"Around the Campfire."*

I dragged my eyes off the painting and looked at Mr. Matthews. I've never seen anyone look as surprised as he did at that moment. "How on earth did you know it was a Bierstadt?" he asked.

I quickly filled Mr. Matthews and Professor Knettle in on our research in the neighborhood and in the library.

I stopped talking, and we all turned and stared at the large painting again. Instead of the ugly barn, we now saw several trappers around a bright campfire. There was a moon partly hiding behind clouds in the sky and tall dark trees everywhere. One man was walking out of the darkness toward the bright orange flames.

I saw what looked like initials in the corner, and I moved in real close and squinted. Although I wasn't sure, I convinced myself that I could make out an "A" and maybe a "B."

Mr. Matthews had cleaned up the old frame, too, and it shone. None of us spoke for a moment. We stood there, staring.

"Gosh!" I finally said. "How could a valuable painting like that turn up in an antique shop in the Sierras and get sold for almost nothing?"

"Although many Bierstadts are in important collections, a few have disappeared from sight," Mr. Matthews said. "At one time, his paintings could have been purchased very cheaply. Sometimes when a person dies, and things are given away or sold out of the house, a painting finds its way to some pretty strange places."

"It was lucky that Judge Winters found it, or that Bierstadt may have sat in the little store for a long, long time," I said.

"Now, we shouldn't get our hopes too high," cautioned Mr. Matthews. "It's definitely a Bierstadt scene. It's *Around the Campfire*, all right. But people make copies of famous pictures all the time. Is it an original? Only an expert in the field can tell us that. But frankly, I'm a pretty cautious man, and I'm quite convinced in my own mind that this is an original Bierstadt. The canvas is the right age."

"How old is it?" I asked.

"Well over a hundred years old. Bierstadt did most of his work between 1860 and 1880. He died in 1902. As you boys have learned, most of his well-known pictures are of famous mountains in the west. In fact, his painting of Yosemite Park hangs in the Metropolitan Museum in New York City."

"Mr. Matthews, what do you think this picture could be worth?" Professor Knettle asked.

"I hesitate to put an exact price on it. Many factors have to be considered. A painting is worth what someone will pay for it, and only a small part of the art-buying public is interested in western landscapes."

"It's a real good picture though," Dynamike said. "It makes you feel like you could warm your hands sitting around that campfire."

"You're right," Mr. Matthews agreed. "But we also need to know more about its condition. Having a coat of paint smeared on it, being stored in a basement, going through a flood, and having a coat of paint removed is not the recommended technique for the care of valuable pictures. In spite of all that, my guess is that if it's an original, it's certainly worth over fifty thousand dollars."

"Wow!" I breathed. "Wow! I knew it was a hidden masterpiece!" I jumped up and was joined by Dynamike and Aaron in high fives.

Aaron stopped celebrating long enough to turn to Mr. Matthews and ask, "And what about the other paintings?"

"I'd forgotten about them," Professor Knettle said. He was looking dazed.

"They're worth forgetting," Mr. Matthews said. "My guess is that there was a group of paintings in an antique shop, and Judge Matthews, who was a very savvy collector, bought the group instead of calling attention to the one picture that he really wanted. He probably wasn't sure it was a Bierstadt and was going to bring it home and verify his suspicions. I'll bet he bought all five of them for very little. From what Wink has told us, it seems the judge didn't mention his hopes of having found a great picture even to his wife, and he died before he ever had a chance to find out if he had discovered a valuable painting or not."

"Wow!" I said. "Wow!" I gazed at the painting again.

"But you'll want an expert opinion on all this," Mr. Matthews said. "I'd say these other four paintings are of no particular value. The oak frames are quite nice, but I don't think there's another masterpiece here. There's no sign of one picture being painted over another."

"I wonder what I should do now," Professor Knettle said. "I really don't know where to start. I have to fly back to Oregon tomorrow. We've got to decide what to do before then."

I sat back down in my chair, and in my most professional voice said, "The WHAM Agency will be glad to help in any way we can."

"Thanks, Wink. It's incredible how much you boys have already helped," Professor Knettle said. "What I think I need next is the name of another art expert who could verify your opinion, Mr. Matthews. Could you suggest someone?"

"I believe the best person to consult about an 1860s western landscape is Robert Boreland at the San Francisco Art Museum," Mr. Matthews said. "He's an old friend. I could phone in the morning and see if he'd be willing to give us an opinion."

"Fine," agreed Professor Knettle. "And, of course, I'd be willing to pay any reasonable fees and expenses that might be involved. Could you arrange to get the painting safely to him?"

"Glad to," agreed Mr. Matthews. "In fact, I'll drive it there myself. I'd be delighted for the chance to talk to Boreland. I haven't seen him in some time now. And perhaps it would be an opportunity for the members of the WHAM Agency to take a short field trip to the museum?"

"Wow!" I said. "That'd be great!" I glanced at Aaron and Dynamike who looked as excited as I felt.

Then I turned to Professor Knettle. "What will you do with the painting if it is a Bierstadt? Keep it or sell it?" As I asked, visions of what fifty thousand dollars would buy went dancing through my head.

"Before I make that decision, Wink, I'll sleep on it."

"Quite right," Dad agreed. "You need some time. But, I'm wondering what you should do with the paintings tonight?"

"Shouldn't the Bierstadt be in a vault?" I asked.

"I have a large walk-in safe at my shop," volunteered Mr. Matthews. "If you'd like, I can drive back there tonight and lock them up until we've had a chance to consult with Mr. Boreland."

"I'd certainly appreciate that," said Professor Knettle.

"Whew!" I said. "That's great! If those paintings were left here tonight, I think we'd all take turns standing guard."

"I'll call Robert Boreland at his home tomorrow and make an appointment as soon as I can." Mr. Matthews shook hands. "I'll keep in touch, Professor Knettle. Here's my card. Feel free to call."

Aaron, Dynamike, and I helped Mr. Matthews move the paintings out to his car. We carried the box of old paintings that had no value and left the Bierstadt to him. It's funny, a couple of days ago, I was dabbing water and paint off that picture and carrying it everywhere. Tonight, I was afraid to touch it. Of course, I knew now that it might be worth fifty thousand dollars.

Just before he left, Mr. Matthews said to me, "I'll phone you just as soon as there are developments. I know you won't want to miss a thing. If Boreland will see me, and your folks agree, we'll be off on a field trip to San Francisco before you know it."

"Thanks, Mr. Matthews," I said.

After Professor Knettle and Mr. Matthews had gone, Aaron and Dynamike and I helped clear away the coffee cups. We left Mom and Dad in the kitchen while we went back into the living room for a WHAM Agency conference.

"Just think," Dynamike said, "if it hadn't been for your leaky basement, Wink, that old painting might have been lost forever."

"I'm glad the hidden masterpiece is uncovered again," I said.

"If it is an original," cautious Aaron reminded me. "We're not sure yet."

After Aaron and Dynamike left, I went to bed. Questions bounced around in my head like kernels of corn in an air popper. Would the expert in San Francisco be willing to look at the picture? Was it really a Bierstadt? Was it worth fifty thousand dollars?

Before I fell asleep, I stared into the darkness and thought about the Bierstadt. Would Professor Knettle keep it or sell it? If it were mine, I knew what I'd do. I'd hang it on the wall right across the room from my bed where I could look at that warm campfire every night before I closed my eyes.

10

I had forgotten all about the class holiday play in my excitement about our trip to the museum. But Mrs. Tilden hadn't. On Monday morning, she asked Allison, "Is the script ready?"

"Yes," Allison replied. "Jo helped me write it." With a satisfied smirk, she strutted up to the front of the room. Before she could start, I stole a quick glance at the clock wishing that it were already ten.

In her loud, piercing voice, Allison read the entire play from beginning to end. As best I could figure out, there was some sort of heat wave at the North Pole brought on by a fire-breathing dragon. Santa and the elves were in a lot of trouble.

"It's certainly original," Mrs. Tilden observed. Leave it to her to find something positive to say. "I want all of you to think about the play tonight. We'll discuss it again tomorrow. There'll be lots of jobs—acting, directing, props, posters, scenery, programs. Remember, everyone in the class participates." Was that a threat or a promise?

>─┼─◆─○─◇─┼─<

Hurrying home with Dynamike and Aaron in mid-morning made me feel guilty. We were ditching school and getting away with it! Imagine, our own private field trip.

As we walked, I asked, "So what do you think of Allison's play?"

"You have to admit, it's different," Aaron said.

"What committee should we volunteer for?" asked Dynamike.

"Not acting," I said quickly. "I don't want hundreds of people staring at me."

"The poster committee wouldn't be bad," Dynamike suggested.

"If we don't volunteer for posters, we might get stuck with something worse," Aaron added.

"Posters we'd probably make at home," I said. "But if we painted scenery, we might get out of class to work on it on the stage."

"Yeah," Dynamike said. "Let's take our chances on scenery."

The rest of the way home, all we could talk about was the Bierstadt painting. Mr. Matthews picked us up at my house right on time and eased us through town and onto the freeway. I could tell from the looks on their faces and the excitement in their voices that Dynamike and Aaron were as jazzed as I was. We were headed for the big city. We stopped for lunch, Mr. Matthews's treat, and then went straight to the museum.

We carried all the paintings carefully, although Mr. Matthews was all but certain that four of them were worthless. Once inside, we walked to a floor filled with offices marked "No Admittance" and "Private." A guard looked us over carefully, listened to Mr. Matthews explain why we were there, and let us through. I felt pretty important.

When we reached Robert Boreland's office, Mr. Matthews introduced us to the western-art expert. He was tall, well over six feet, and his head was shiny bald with a fringe of silvered-brown hair around the sides and back. We carefully set the paintings down and shook hands. I gave Mr. Boreland our WHAM Agency card.

We stood and watched as Mr. Boreland cut the strings and removed the wrappings. He glanced quickly at the four old paintings, and not a flicker of interest crossed his face. Then he picked up the Bierstadt. I found myself holding my breath as I watched. A transformation came over him. His face lit up like a little kid who has just been given a triple-decker ice cream cone.

"Well, well, well," he finally said. "Will you look at this." He peered at the initials in the corner, and, if possible, he looked happier still after staring at them.

"Unless I'm very much mistaken, it's just as you suspected," Mr. Boreland said. "I think we have a Bierstadt on our hands."

Whoosh! All the breath I'd been holding came rushing out. "A real Bierstadt?" I managed to ask.

"I feel almost sure of it," he said. "Of course it will take a little time to authenticate it, but I'll call you just as soon as I finish my complete examination." He paused to smile at us. "Mr. Matthews has told me all about your investigation, and I must say that I'm very impressed you boys could uncover the artist on your own."

He shook hands with all of us. As we walked out of the office, I felt a thrill run down my spine. This was big! This was historical! The Hidden Masterpiece was now in the San Francisco Art Museum.

><-+-<>-+-O-+-<>-+-<

About eight o'clock that night, our phone rang. I snatched it up. It was Mr. Matthews.

"Hello, Wink. I just got a call from Mr. Boreland. I've got news for you." He paused. "It turns out I was wrong."

"Wrong?" I croaked. I felt as if someone had poured a bucket of ice water over me. No, no, I silently screamed. Wrong? Wrong? You can't be wrong!

"Yes, I'm afraid so. You know how I told you that if the painting were a Bierstadt, it might be worth forty or fifty thousand dollars? Well, Mr. Boreland says there's no question about it. It's an original Bierstadt painting all right, and even though it's not in perfect condition, he estimates its worth about $500,000."

For a few seconds, I was too stunned to say anything. Finally, I managed a "Wow!" I felt like I'd been in a free-fall from an airplane and my parachute just opened.

"I knew we had a masterpiece on our hands."

"What about the other four paintings?"

"He doesn't think they have any value. Frankly, I knew they were worthless, but for Professor Knettle's sake, I had to be positive. Mr. Boreland will report again when he's absolutely sure."

"Where's the Bierstadt right now?"

"Mr. Boreland's keeping it safe in the museum. I'll phone Professor Knettle with the news, but it may be a few weeks before we get final results on all the tests. Then Professor Knettle can decide what he's going to do with them all."

"Thanks, Mr. Matthews."

"It's you who deserves thanks, Wink. You and the WHAM Agency. You had faith in that painting, and you boys weren't about to give up until you'd solved your mystery. Identifying it in the library took skill and hard work."

"Thanks, Mr. Matthews. It took some luck, too."

I hung up and called Aaron and Dynamike to share the news. Then I went running to find Mom and Dad.

"I've got to hand it to you, Wink," Mom said after I'd spilled the news. "From the first you were sure it was an art treasure."

"All private investigators have a special sixth sense," I said proudly.

"I'm going over to talk with Mr. Jensen," Dad said. "He's been checking with the city attorney about Professor Knettle's purchases from the Winters's estate to make sure that everything is legal, and that he's the undisputed owner. Want to come?"

"Sure."

When we got there, Mr. Jensen told us that since Professor Knettle bought the pictures at an open sale, there were no strings attached as far as the city attorney was concerned. The paintings, whether they were old barns or masterpieces, were his.

"Professor Knettle has clear title to the paintings," Mr. Jensen said. "What a lucky guy. His twenty-five dollars could bring him half a million."

"Gee, Mr. Jensen," I said. "What do you think he'll do with the Bierstadt?"

"My guess is, he'll sell it."

When we got back home, I said, "I wish I knew for sure what Professor Knettle was going to do with all the paintings. The mystery's not over till we know that. But it's wait, wait, wait again. I've sure had a lot of practice at that lately."

"Practice makes perfect," Mom teased. "And that goes for math, too. Don't you have homework tonight?"

"Oh," I groaned. Reluctantly I stopped thinking about paintings and started thinking about fractions.

>─┼─◆─◦─◦─◦─┼─◄

At school the next afternoon, Mrs. Tilden called our class meeting to order. "Any comments or suggestions about the play?"

No one spoke. Bury it, would be my suggestion, but I didn't dare say that out loud.

"All right," Mrs. Tilden said. "We're going to need a director, actors, backstage helpers, a prompter, and people for make-up, posters, costumes, scenery building, and props." As she spoke, Mrs. Tilden wrote the job titles on the chalkboard. "Questions?"

"When will we give the play, Mrs. Tilden?" Jo asked.

"The day before winter vacation. We'll give it twice, once in the morning and once in the afternoon. That way there'll be plenty of room for all the classes that want to come watch. We'll invite your parents and friends to attend either show."

"Now the most important position," Mrs. Tilden continued, "is that of the director. As soon as we select one, I'll turn the meeting over to that person. Would anyone like to suggest the name of someone to be the director of our show?"

Jo raised her hand. "I'd like to suggest Allison. She worked hard on the committee that wrote the script."

Mrs. Tilden wrote Allison's name on the chalkboard. Then someone suggested Jo's name and Mrs. Tilden wrote it. "Anyone else? Okay. Let's take a vote. I suggest that the girl with the most votes be director and the runner-up be the assistant director. I know both Jo and Allison would do a good job, and together, they'll be great. I'll hand out slips of paper. Please write only one name, either Allison or Jo."

Three kids went up front to tabulate the results. Jo won. Apparently I wasn't the only one who found Allison bossy.

Jo chose her actors and committee chairpersons from volunteers who raised their hands. She was friendly but business-like, and I was glad she'd won.

"Now, who wants to be the dragon?" asked Jo. No hands went up. All the eager ones had signed up for either major acting roles or the committee chairpersons.

"What?" asked Mrs. Tilden who had been standing at the side of the room. She pretended disbelief as the silence lengthened. "You mean to tell me that no one in our class wants to play a fierce, fire-breathing dragon? "

Still no hands went up.

"Do I need to choose someone for this dangerous assignment?" teased Mrs. Tilden.

There was still no response.

"I think I know what the problem is," she said. "No one feels big enough for the part. Maybe it is too much for one person. I'd like to suggest that Aaron be the head of the dragon, Wink the body, and Mike bring up the tail. How's that?"

The class laughed and burst into applause while the three of us sat there in astonishment. Then everyone signed up for the various committees.

As I walked home with Dynamike and Aaron that afternoon, I asked, "How did this happen? One minute we were sitting there quietly minding our own business, and the next minute we were tricked into dragon parts. Why us?"

Aaron laughed. "I guess Mrs. Tilden recognizes talent. Not just anyone could play the dragon, you know."

"Cheer up," advised Dynamike. "At least we're all in it together."

And we soon found out how right Dynamike was. The dragon costume was a king-sized sheet, dyed a brilliant green, attached to a papier-mâché head. Styrofoam spikes ran down the backbone, ending in a single, bumpy row from an egg carton. When we climbed into the various sections and got our eye holes arranged so we could see, we made quite a beast.

Everyone had fun at rehearsals. Jo reminded people to speak loudly and managed to get us in position so that we stopped bumping into each other. After Santa has his talk with the fire-breathing dragon, who obligingly puts out his fire, there are more problems. The elves, Santa, and Mrs. Claus discover they have so many presents to deliver this year that the sleigh is too heavy, and the reindeer can't take off. It's dragon to the

rescue! The friendly dragon is hitched to the sleigh, spreads his gigantic wings, and helps out the reindeer.

At this moment in the play, I spread out the wings of green tissue paper fashioned around wire frames, which up until then were held close to the body. The result was pretty dramatic.

Since Aaron was the head of the dragon, he had to learn and speak all the lines. Even though he was short, Dynamike still was in an uncomfortable position, sort of hunched-down at the tail. So all in all, I felt pretty good about being in the middle. I'd lucked out. All I had to do was flap my arms.

We presented the play on the morning of December 21, the last day of school before winter break. Things went smoothly, but it wasn't easy for the three of us to move in a coordinated way. Allison's walkie-talkies would have helped so that our dragon head could communicate with our tail.

My folks said they'd be at the afternoon show, and Mrs. Carabell was coming, too. I was too busy trying to see where I was going and working the wings to take a peek into the audience to find them. Afterwards, I spotted them in the hall.

"It was wonderful, Wink," Mom and Dad said.

"That play put everyone into the holiday spirit," Mrs. Carabell added. "And thanks to you, I'll have a wonderful Christmas surrounded by Fortune and her kittens."

"Thanks. I'm glad you liked it." I felt kind of embarrassed standing there, so I said, "I have to hurry now and help clean up before our party."

"Come straight home after school," Mom said. "I've made an appointment for you."

I had already turned and started to leave, but when I heard the ominous word "appointment," I stopped and faced Mom again. "An appointment? With the dentist? This afternoon? No fair. Not a dragon and a dentist in one day!"

Mom laughed, and Dad said, "Not with the dentist, Wink. Professor Knettle will be at our house waiting to talk with you."

"He will?" This was the first I'd heard about this. "Okay. Can Aaron and Dynamike come, too?"

"Sure," Dad said. "Be sure to ask them. We want them there."

I ran to help with the clean up. When we got back to class, we had a cast and crew party. Then Mrs. Tilden sent us on our way to a two-week vacation by handing us each a candy cane as we rushed out the door.

Dynamike, Aaron, and I ran all the way home and into my house where Bugle greeted us with wild tail wagging. We hurried into the living room. What a crowd! Mom and Dad were sitting there with Professor Knettle, Mr. Jensen, Mr. Matthews, a man with a big flash camera, and another man and woman who I didn't recognize.

As soon as he saw us, Mr. Matthews said, "Here's the young man who first uncovered the mysterious masterpiece. This is Wink." He stood and put an arm on my shoulder. Then he turned toward my buddies and said, "And these two young men are the other members of

134

the WHAM Agency, Aaron and Mike. They interviewed neighbors, did research, and found out on their own that the old painting in the basement was a valuable Bierstadt!"

I smiled kind of stupidly, wondering who all these people were.

"Aaron, Mike, and Wink, I'd like to have you meet the mayor of Santa Rosa, Mr. John Brust, and the Director of the Winters Library Building Fund, Ms. Martha Mills." Then he pointed at the man with the camera and said, "And this is Jim Johnson, a photojournalist with *The Santa Rosa Tribune*."

"Hi," I said, nodding in their general direction and suddenly feeling very awkward. Aaron and Dynamike mumbled "hello," too.

"I wanted you all here when I signed these papers," Professor Knettle said, "because you've all had a part in this mystery. Although they aren't worth anything, my wife and I have decided to keep the four old paintings as souvenirs. But we think it's only fair to make a gift of the Bierstadt to the mayor of the city of Santa Rosa so he can sell it and add the money to the Winters Library Building Fund."

"On behalf of the city, let me say we're terribly grateful," said the mayor.

As I tried to take in this new turn of events, the photographer began arranging us for a picture around the dining room table. Professor Knettle, pen poised over an official-looking document, sat in the middle, with the mayor on one side and the Library Building Fund

Director on the other. Aaron, Dynamike, and I stood right behind Professor Knettle.

We watched as Professor Knettle signed the papers. I felt a surge of pride as the mayor made a little speech pointing out we'd saved this painting for posterity as well as helped the town get a new branch library.

"This will make a great story," the photographer said, scribbling notes and taking several more shots. "Hidden Masterpiece Found by Local Private Investigators." I realized we were about to become famous. Fortunately at this point I also remembered to reach in my back pocket and hand him one of our WHAM Agency cards. This could be good for business!

"We've already been in touch with Robert Boreland," Ms. Mills added. "He expects the San Francisco Art Museum to make the city a handsome offer for the painting. It will hang in an excellent gallery where people can enjoy it.

"And," she added as she looked around and smiled, "with this money, our fund-raising campaign will go over the top! We'll be able to build the Winters Branch Library next year."

"Wow!" I said, exchanging high fives with Aaron and Dynamike. "Thanks, Professor Knettle. What a Christmas present for the city of Santa Rosa!"

Watching everyone talking and smiling at once, I thought—who knows, maybe the WHAM Agency will use that new library one day to help solve another case.